Table of Contents

2015

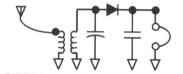
A Further Change of Pace
By Dan Petersen, W7OIL

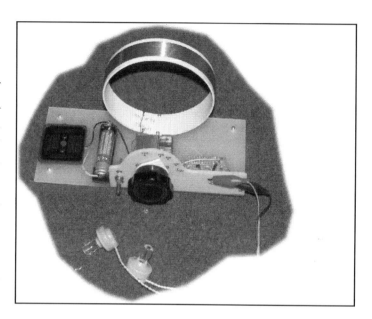

Speeding through the cosmos the unshielded nuclear furnace was operational and had been for a long time. A power greater than mankind was running this behemoth and there was absolutely nothing this fragile, puny thing called "man" could do about it. Yet without this immense furnace mankind would soon perish. Yes, friends, I speak of our sun, a dwarf main-sequence star in an ordinary section of the mundane Milky Way galaxy. The sun provides life itself and will continue to do so if we don't blow ourselves to smithereens first. Barring heat generated inside the Earth it provides us with ALL our energy. We only need to find ways to harvest this energy for our essential needs, like i-phones, electric toothbrushes and top-end Hummers.

The sun also provides the source for the operation of the "solar cell". In 1839, A. E. Becquerel discovered that certain materials such as selenium would generate an electrical current when exposed to light. This remained pretty much a laboratory curiosity with only limited applications until the ubiquitous Bell Laboratories developed the first practical silicon solar cell in 1954. Nowadays you find them everywhere, from immense arrays powering entire buildings to solar powered yard lights. What a coincidence, mentioning solar yard lights. This article revolves around an alternate use of the solar yard light – a solar radio receiver.

'Way back in July, 2012 I wrote an article called "A Change of Pace", which detailed the construction of an MK-484 AM receiver. I was rather pleased with the performance of such a simple circuit so I decided to return to the radio bench and make a good receiver better. Not in performance but in the way it is powered.

Enter the solar yard light. When I first thought of using a solar cell to keep a battery charged in this receiver my thoughts drifted into the retail realm of over-the-counter cells. Radio Shack sells such but I was put off by the price. My "Raised-by-Great Depression-era-parents" mind quickly shifted gears (do you smell burnt metal?) for other sources. I was in a hardware store (I won't mention Ace's name) and saw some solar yard lights on sale. At about $3.00 and some slight modifications (i.e. tear it apart) you could have a solar cell and a battery with holder at your disposal! I picked one up and brought it home.

Figure 1 shows the complete light. I have had several different types of these lights and I found with all of them the top removes with a twist of the top. You feel it turn and stop – then the top comes off. Inside there is an LED in the center and four small screws holding the top together. Remove these screws and the two halves come apart. Figure 2 shows the "guts" of this unit. Inside you will find

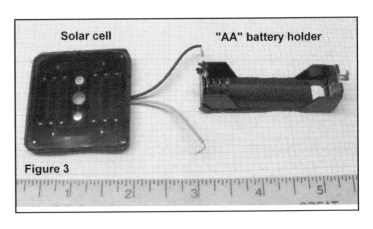

Solar cell   "AA" battery holder

Figure 3

a battery (usually nickel/cadmium) a circuit board driver circuit for the LED and the solar cell on the other half. The solar cell should be called more correctly a "solar panel" as it has several solar cells in series – four in most yard lights. Since each cell generates 0.5 volts DC in full sun, that equates to 0.5v times 4 cells = 2.0 vdc. This one had eight – two banks of four. I measured the charging current into the NiCd battery (in full sun) and found it charges at over 25 milliamperes. Since the receiver draws about one milliampere when "on" the charge rate is more than sufficient!

I applied some "bandsaw technology" to the top of the yard light, cutting out the solar panel and the battery holder. The LED circuit card I put away for some other future hare-brained project. I sanded

Solar yard light

The stuff you want is inside the top.

Figure 1

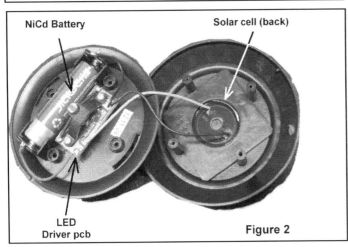

NiCd Battery   Solar cell (back)

LED
Driver pcb   Figure 2

the edges smooth, making them ready for assembly. Figure 3 shows the finished product.

Now for the Receiver.

I took my old project from the July, 2012 article and ruthlessly took it apart. I say ruthlessly because there is nobody here named Ruth. "Ruth"lessly" – Get it….

Ahem - Why use more materials to make an almost identical set when all the stuff is there already? This receiver is novel in that it uses a small loop antenna to receive radio signals. Figure 4 shows the schematic of the receiver. L1 and C1 comprise the tuned circuit for the receiver. L1 is wound on a one-inch wide piece of 4-inch PVC drain pipe. It needs to be mounted in the vertical dimension. If mounted horizontally it will not "cut" any magnetic lines of force and you will not hear anything. Think of it as the secondary of a giant RF transformer, with the broadcast station as the primary and the distance between as the "core". The MK484 receives the tuned signal from the tuned circuit, where it is amplified 70dB (ten million times) by three RF amplifiers, then detected to extract the audio. This audio, along with an "AGC" voltage presented at pin 3 supplies the audio to a crystal earphone. Down in the lower right of Figure 4 you will see the battery and "SC1". SC1 is the solar panel, connected in parallel with the battery. One caution is that, if you store the radio in the dark for a long time, i.e. months or longer, take the battery out. When dark there is a VERY small reverse current flowing through the solar panel, similar to the reverse current through a silicon diode. Tiny but there and it will eventually drain the battery. Also, when constructing the circuit place C3 as close as possible to pin 3 of the MK-484. Even ½ inch away from the MK-484 can be too far! Otherwise the layout is not critical.

Figure 5 shows the positioning of the solar panel and the battery. Nickel/Cadmium batteries seem to be the norm in these yard lights and I have found that, in time, the "NiCd" battery will "memorize" itself to death. NiCd's have a nasty habit of "memorizing" a charge/discharge cycle and will eventually become non-functional. Cold weather doesn't help the process either. Nickel-Metal Hydride (NiMH) batteries do not have this problem and, in theory, should last a lot longer.

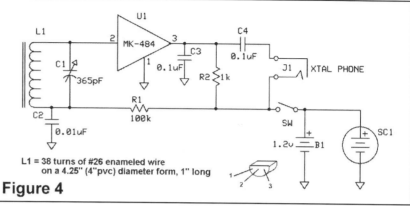

Figure 4

L1 = 38 turns of #26 enameled wire on a 4.25" (4"pvc) diameter form, 1" long

Figure 6 reveals how the "radio" part of the receiver is arranged. The tuning coil is mounted behind the tuning capacitor and seems to be far enough away from the tuning knob that "hand capacity" is not a problem. The MK-484 circuit is on a small piece of perforated bakelite and is mounted to the "chassis" with a single screw and standoff. The "chassis" and "front panel" are made from "Lexan" colored plastic. I get scrap Lexan from the "Tap" plastics store in Portland, Oregon. I find it interesting the changes in people's tastes over the years. In the early '90s the scraps tended to bright colors while today colors are fairly uncommon.

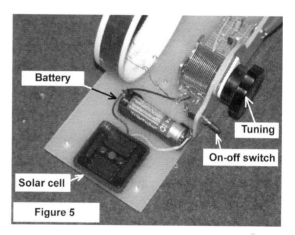

Figure 5

The receiver is pretty easy to use. It drives a pair of crystal earphones connected in parallel at a pleasant volume. The AGC appears to work to minimize distortion from local flamethrowers. Too bad they can't minimize the bucket-mouth crock-jocks too! There are two music stations in my area that I pick up and one of them even has identifiable music!

This is a fun little project that had enough innovation to help retain my last remaining brain-cell. A radio like this would appeal to the Armageddon-fearing survivalist as well. Of course there will probably be no stations to listen TO – but that's another story.

Be creative and make me proud of you!

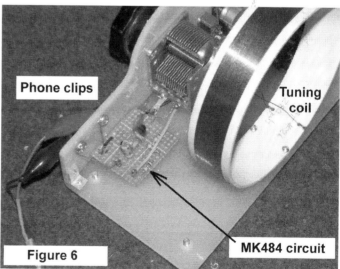

Figure 6

My Spider Web Crystal Set
By Uncle Phil, WØXI

This set was fun to build and is great to listen to. It sounds so good that it's pulled me away from some 20-meter CW and 2-meter FM activity; and the FT-1900-RL is a new rig! Maybe I need to head back to the grocery store and get a dozen Nathen's Hot Dogs! They go well with CW QSOs!

This crystal set started as my completed AM Antenna Tuner Kit, my JFET AM Crystal Set Kit and my 50 foot half-vertical and half horizontal in the attic antenna. With these in hand, I decided – finally – to NC punch some spider web coil forms, as per the picture and see how they'd do instead of the usual PVC cylindricals. Turns out they did great as expected, particularly the one wound with 150/45 Litz wire, shown in the back in the picture and installed in the JFET AM Crystal Set. More Litz, as we all know, begets more Q; and, more Q begets more selectivity and more volume! Yea!

The first spider I wound used #22 enamel wire. It's shown in the foreground. The Q is not as high as it would be with Litz but the wire is cheaper. However, this is not a problem in that the antenna ground return resistance is nearly 250 ohms. As they say in Jersey, "Fo Git About It!" I could have used a molded coil with a slug and it wouldn't have made any difference. But I wanted the "Tuggle" style antenna tuner's coil to match that in the main set shape wise so decided it was a keeper. The spider Litz coil in the crystal set is remarkable. I noticed that my selectivity improved nearly 50% from what it was with the old PVC baby in there. This spider has 56 turns, an inner diameter of 1.6 inches and an outer diameter of 4.2 inches, with the Litz wire diameter at 0.023 inches (150/4 Litz).

For you formula jockeys – yup that includes Herby, WR9H – here's the equation for the spider web coil, a modified Wheeler,

$$L(uH) = \frac{N^2 A^2}{30A - 11D_I} \text{ and } A = \frac{D_I + N(w+s)}{2}$$

where D_I = inner diameter in inches, w = wire diameter,

s = distance between windings, N = no. of turns, D_O = outer diameter.

My final mod to date was to change the source resistor in the JFET detector from 1k to 22K and the drain resistor to 2.2k. This forced the JFET into its linear region, causing Dr. Distortion to take a hike when listening to strong stations. It just sounds great, with weak or strong signals! I also noted, with the antenna tuner in line and listening during the afternoon, that WIBW at 580 kHz, sports radio KC at 610, WHB KC at 810, and my local 500 watt flame thrower, KLWN at 1320, were all loud with good audio! Can't wait to listen late into the night to see how the 50K guys like WGN Chicago sound! 73s.

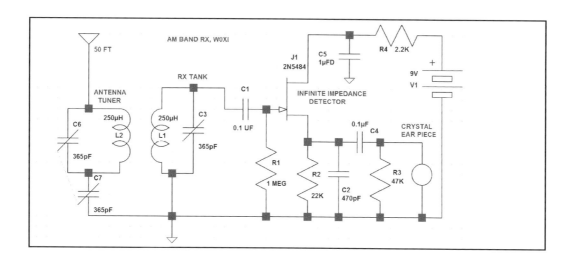

The Spider Web (or Spiral) Coil
by Phil Anderson, WØXI

When winding coils you have a number of form choices: standard cylindrical, basket weave, spider or donut (on a ferrite core). Any one of the first three forms works nicely in pairs when you want to add an antenna tuner to your crystal set. In this piece our focus is the spider web coil. A 250 uH spider web coil using 150/45 Litz wire wound on an ABS plastic form is shown in picture 1. Why use the spider? We think it's easy to wind and works as good as a basket weave.

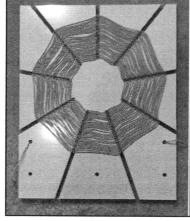

Picture 1

Spider web and basket weave coils will produce a stronger signal than their cousin, the standard close wound cylindrical, for a given input signal. This is accomplished by separating adjacent windings by the thickness of one winding. This separation reduces the proximity effect between wires, wherein the closer they are a current in one will increase the resistance of the other.

The separation of adjacent turns is accomplished by breaking up each full turn into an odd number of segments wherein each additional segment is wound on the opposite side of a thin flat form. This is enabled by cutting an odd-number of radial slits extending outward from the outer edge of the internal circular center.

Windings of the first few turns are displayed in picture 2. The winding starts from the back of the interior center; hence the first and all odd segments of the first turn will show on the top side as noted by "1." The last segment of turn 1, segment 9, comes out on top and zig-zags over to become turn 2, where it goes underneath the form again. The following segment of turn 2 is then on the top as noted, and so on.

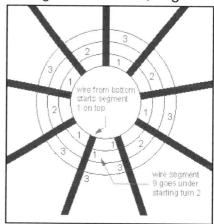

Picture 2

The inductance of the spider coil is determined by its inner and outer diameters and the diameter and spacing of the wire, as defined in picture 3. The picture displays what you would see if you cut all the wires in one of the radial slits and removed one of the segments of the form. From this side view, you would see the turns alternately wound on top and bottom of the form as the coil builds up from the inner radius. Note that a flat spiral would

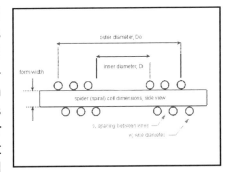

have the same dimensions but all the wires would be on top of the form. Given that the width (thickness) of the form is generally a bit greater than the diameter of the wire but much less than the outer diameter of the coil, the spider coil approaches the same dimensions as a flat spiral coil wound on one side of the form. Thus, the equation for the spiral coil can be used when winding the spider coil.

The equation for the spider coil is

$$L(uH) = \frac{N^2 A^2}{30A - 11D_I} \text{ and } A = \frac{D_I + N(w+s)}{2}$$

where D_I = inner diameter in inches, w = wire diameter, s = distance between windings, N = no. of turns, D_O = outer diameter.

If you wish to use an on-line calculator go here: http://www.deepfriedneon.com/tesla_f_calcspiral.html, assuming that it is still posted there.

Table 1 lists our calculation results for four 250 uH coils using different sizes and types of wire. The results for the 150/45 Litz wire coil, also shown in picture 1, specify that given that wire, that form with 9 slits, an inner diameter of 1.6 inches, an

outer diameter of 4.2 inches and 56 turns, the inductance should be 254 uH. We tested the coil on the bench and the results matched another 250 uH cylindrical coil on hand.

Happy winding!

Appendix:
Some may be curious about the origin of the spider/spiral equation. It has been said that it is derived – a better word might be rearranged – from Harold Wheeler's equation for a cylindrical coil. That idea seems plausible given the following. Ask yourself this question, "When is a coil both a cylindrical and a spider?" The answer is a single loop of wire as noted by coils A & B in picture 4. Second, what might the inductance of coils C and D be, given that they have the same number of turns and the diameter of C is equal to the average diameter of the turns of D? It would seem that the total flux produced by each would be the same!

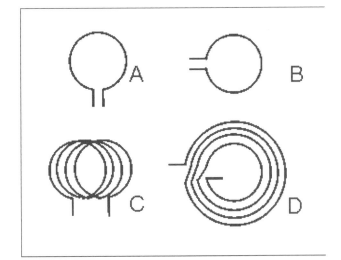

Starting with 250 uH spiral coils,

wire type	inner diameter	N turns	wire dia	turn spacing	outer dia	length wire	L uH	wire feet
hookup	1.6	51	0.03	0.02	6.7	664	251	55
#22	1.6	56	0.025	0	4.4	527	257	44
150/45	1.6	56	0.023	0	4.176	508	254	42
#26	1.6	51	0.016	0	3.4	439	246	37

For The Electronics Beginner
By Xtal Staff

OHM's LAW

Most electronic equipment consists of a power supply or battery, transistors or ICs, connectors, a case, and three types of passive components called resistors, capacitors, and coils (inductors). This note covers the basics about the resistor.

George Ohm wrote a paper in 1826 describing the relationship between the voltage applied across a resistor and the resulting current flowing through it. In honor of his early works, we call this relationship Ohm's Law. The law can be expressed as a ratio as follows,

$$\frac{V}{I} = R,$$ where V is the voltage in volts, I the current in amperes, and R is the resistance in ohms.

For most resistors, R is a constant. The value of R depends upon the resistivity of the material used and its size and shape.

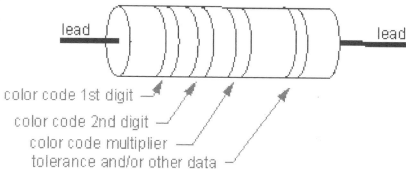

the resistor... its value is noted by the color code

Resistors that you can purchase from a retail outlet, such as Mouser on line, vary in size. A common physical size is the ¼-watt carbon film resistor noted in the drawing. Manufacturers make resistors in a range of standard values, using two digits and multiplier and these are represented by three color bands printed on the resistor as noted in the drawing.

For example, a 100 ohm resistor is represented by brown (1) and black (0) color bands plus a multiplier of brown (10). We interpret this brown-black-brown color code as 10 times 10 or 100 ohms. The full range of color codes and multipliers is shown in the table.

Now let's check out the color code for a much larger resistor, say 220k ohms. What's k stand for? It's an abbreviation for 1000 and is used to avoid writing a bunch of zeroes. For example, 220k is the same as writing 220,000 but we avoid writing all those zeroes. This is common practice for experienced hobbyists and techs. Now let's map out the color code. We need RED for the first 2, RED for the second 2 and YELLOW for the four zeroes needed (note that 0 and k is the same thing as 4 zeroes and therefore pick yellow).

	A	B	C	D
1				
2			RESISTOR COLOR CODES	
3		COLOR	SIGNIFICANT	DECIMAL
4			FIGURE	MULTIPLIER
5		BLACK	0	1
6		BROWN	1	10
7		RED	2	100
8		ORANGE	3	1000
9		YELLOW	4	10000
10		GREEN	5	100000
11		BLUE	6	1000000
12		VIOLET	7	10000000
13		GREY	8	100000000
14		WHITE	9	1000000000
15		GOLD		0.1
16		SILVER		0.01
17				
18		Examples: A 2.2K resistor code = RED, RED, RED = 2200.		
19		A 10 ohm resistor code = BROWN, BLACK, BROWN		
20				

An Application

Now that you know how the resistors are color coded, let's attach a resistor to a 1.5 volt battery and use Ohm's Law to determine how much current and power the resistor will demand.

$$\frac{V}{I} = R \text{ rearranged is}$$

$$I = \frac{V}{R} = \frac{1.5}{10k} = \frac{1.5}{10,000} = 0.00015 \text{ amperes} = 0.15 \text{ ma.}$$

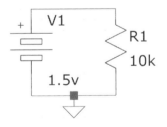

When the battery voltage is applied to a resistor, a current flows through the resistor and back to the ground lead of the battery. Rearranging the equation for Ohm's Law introduced at the beginning, we can solve for the current heating up the resistor.

10k represents 10,000 ohms since k represents 1,000 ohms so the current is 0.00015 amperes. Circuit designers prefer to work with numbers that have fewer zeroes so convert the amperes to milli-amperes, abbreviated as ma.

The power consumed in a resistor is obtained by multiplying the voltage across it by the current through it or by squaring the current and multiplying it by the resistance. The former is easier in this example. So, multiplying 0.15 ma times 1.5 volts gives us the power consumed in the resistor of 0.225 milli-watts (mw).

Mounting/Installing the 365 PF Air-Variable Capacitor
By Xtal Staff

The range of this capacitance is approximately 15 to 390 pf, as measured with a BK Precision 810C capacitance meter. The cap can be mounted to a front panel or placed on a chassis, with the shaft extending through the panel or mounted with the 365 L-bracket. The front panel of the capacitor has two 6-32 tapped holes at top-left and right. The bottom has four 6-32 tapped holes for chassis mounting. The frame is U-shaped, thus supplying the front and back of the cap housing. The rotor plates are grounded to the chassis via the shaft. The stator plates connect to two-solder lugs on each side via two small phenolic boards.

Electrical connection to the chassis/rotor plates is accomplished by attaching a wire to a solder lug installed on the front panel or base of the cap frame, as shown in pictures 1 and 2. For front panel connection, a 6-32 hex nut is added with the lug so that the 6-32 by ¼ screw does not extend into the interior of the cap and thus block full rotation of the rotor plates. Alternatively, you can add the solder lug to the bottom of the cap, thus allowing for panel mounting from the front of the capacitor. Note that the front plate of the cap has a bit of a bulge around the shaft to hold it and the bearings in place. Because of this, you'll want to drill a third hole in your front panel to accommodate for that.

Picture 1

Picture 2 shows the bottom of the cap. Two screws, added diagonally, are sufficient to hold it in place. Of course, for chassis mounting, the

Picture 2

solder lug would not be used, just two 6-32 by ¼ screws – from the bottom and thru the chassis – and two washers or a "spacer plate" (see picture 3) on top of the chassis but under the cap, so that the screw does not extend too far into the interior of the capacitor body and thereby short the plates.

Picture 3

The Vertical 365 Mounting bracket will allow you to mount the cap above the chassis platform and away from the front panel. Holes at the bottom of this L-shaped bracket (shown in picture 4) can be used to mount to the chassis; and, the two small vertical slots are provided for 6-32 by 1/4 screws to secure the cap to the bracket. Adjust height as desired.

Picture 4

Mounting/Installing a 6-1 Reduction Drive
By Xtal Staff

The pictures show a 6-1 reduction drive attached to the shaft of a 365 air variable capacitor. The front panel has been removed so you can see the knob attached to the shaft of the reduction drive.

A good way to approach the installation of this combination is to slip the ¼-in opening of the reduction drive shaft onto the shaft of the capacitor, as noted in pictures 1 and 2, securing it lightly with the two screws provided in the brass shaft. Then place the combination on the chassis so the shaft at the far right sticks out enough from the front panel to accommodate a knob. Then slip the L-bracket on the reduction drive at the front so the larger portion of the L-bracket is vertical and flush with the tabs of the drive sticking out horizontally on each side. Secure the bracket and drive together with two 4-40 by 3/8th screws and two hex nuts. Finally, using a pencil, mark the chassis through the two holes on the bottom of the L-bracket and remove the assembly to drill out the holes. Use a 5/32 or 11/64 drill bit to leave a little slack in the holes.

Picture 1

Now you are ready to secure the combination and reattach the front panel. Use two 6-32 by ¼ inch screws to secure the capacitor, inserting them in a diagonal pattern from the bottom of the chassis, through the chassis, through the spacer, and screw into two of the four holes on the bottom of the capacitor. This takes a bit of jiggling to get started. Then secure the bottom of the L-bracket holding the reduction drive with 4-40 by 3/8 or ¼ screws and secure on the bottom of the chassis with hex nuts. Finally, level the tabs on the reduction drive and tighten the nut and screw combination located on each side.

If you compare the tension on the knob with a 365 capacitor with 8-1 internal reduction drive to that of a 365 with external drive, you will notice that the later will be a bit more stiff.

Picture 2

The MK484 AM Radio "Mini" Kit

By Phil Anderson, WØXI

This "mini" kit is a subset of the original MK484 AM RADIO KIT and uses a small portion of the printed circuit board (PCB) of that kit. The "MINI" features the MK484 integrated circuit (IC), a ferrite rod antenna, a 1.5 volt regulator IC, a handful of resistors and capacitors, a switch, a variable capacitor, a panel and chassis, and a crystal radio ear piece. The set does not need an antenna or a ground since it includes a 3 by 0.5 inch ferrite rod antenna; and, the crystal ear piece takes the place of the usual headphones. The radio tunes the AM band. If you wish to use the MINI with 8-ohm headphones, a bag of parts is available for purchase that includes the 386 audio amplifier IC, volume pot and extra resistors and capacitors required.

Picture 1 is a top view of the PCB that includes the parts needed for the mini kit. You'll note that just 15 parts are added to the board. Leads for a 9V battery clip are shown at the left. We've looped the leads through two holes to form a strain relief, thus giving these wires a longer life time. A power on/off switch is shown at bottom left (not shown in the schematic). The regulator IC, a resistor, and the Led are just to the right. When you press the switch in the LED will light, reminding you to turn it off after listening to save the battery. Jack Expert will tell you that all that is needed there is a 1.5 volt battery. While true, by adding the 1.5 regulator you can make use of those half-used 9V batteries you

likely have in your junk box! The remaining resistors, capacitors and the MK484 IC are all in the middle of the board.

The schematic for the MINI is shown in picture 2. The heart of the radio is, of course, the MK484 integrated circuit. Featured inside the chip are three stages of RF amplification, an automatic gain control (AGC) circuit, biasing and an AM detector. The output at pin 3 will supply about 40 to 50 ma of current to drive the crystal ear piece shown at top-right. The 3.0 by 0.5 inch ferrite rod (L1) and 365 air variable capacitor (C1) – shown at upper left – make up the tuned circuit. A knob is attached to the shaft of the capacitor and is used for

Picture 1

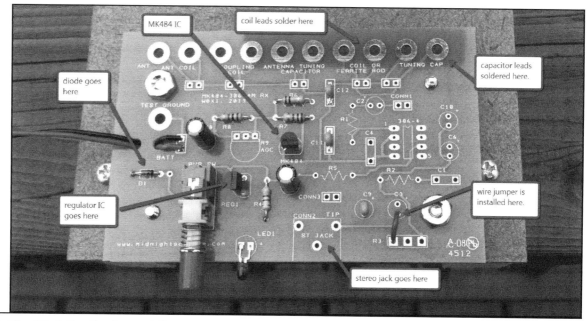

station tuning. The circuitry across the bottom of the schematic includes an LED, power switch, battery connections, and a 1.5 volt regular IC.

Perhaps the neatest thing about the MINI is the pickup coil, wound on the ferrite rod and suspended above the chassis by nylon hardware. No external antenna or ground rod is required for operation. (See picture 3) And my favorite feature: the coil is super simple to wind and secure to the rod with the nylon clamps. I've found it easiest to wind the coil by holding the spool or length of wire between my knees, the left end of the coil assembly with my left hand and turning the rod assembly with my right hand. Each 360 degree turn adds one turn to the coil. The mini requires 60 turns in all. I also found that keeping a slight bit of tension on the wire while winding helps keep the windings taut and tightly spaced.

A 3.5mm stereo jack for the PCB and a 3.5mm mono plug are included with the mini. This makes connection and storage convenient for the ear piece. Plug assembly is shown in picture 4.

The mounting of the 365 air-variable capacitor is a bit unusual. I opted to mount it directly to the front panel while at the same time isolating the metal panel from it, using nylon screws, hex nuts, and washers. (See picture 5)

Picture 2

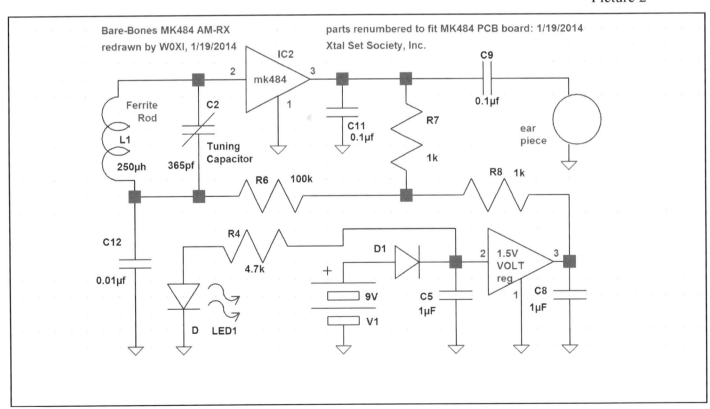

Installation and Operation

A 9V battery is installed in a metal battery clip at the back of the chassis. The only other thing to do is to plug in your ear piece, press the power button and tune to the desired station in the AM band. Since the MK484 IC automatically adjusts volume there is no need for a volume control. By using a ferrite rod for the coil form, no outside antenna or ground is required. You simply tune the knob attached to the variable capacitor to select stations available. Keep in mind that ferrite rod coils are directional, which can be an advantage. For example, if you wish to see if you can pick up a station east of you, orient the ends of the rod north and south.

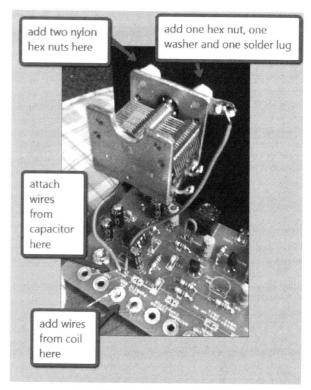

add two nylon hex nuts here

add one hex nut, one washer and one solder lug

attach wires from capacitor here

add wires from coil here

Picture 5

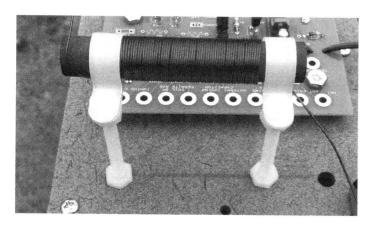

Picture 3

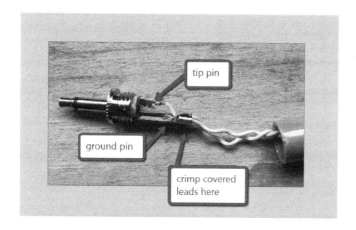

tip pin

ground pin

crimp covered leads here

Picture 4

My Spouse Sends Perfect: "S," "H," and "5" Morse Characters!
Uncle Phil, WØXI

You see, I discovered this while wiring up my first spider-web crystal set in the basement. An aside, I thought this spider web would provide company for the real ones here and there in the corners. My spider coil is shown in the picture 1. It consists of 55 turns of #22 AWG enamel wire wound on a 1/8th inch thick 5 by 6 inch piece of ABS plastic. The inner diameter of the coil is about 1.5 inches and the outside diameter is about 4.5. Total inductance turns out to be about 250 uH, perfect for an AM band crystal set.

My AM band antenna runs 20 feet up to the peak of the roof and then another 20 feet into the attic via the vent, east-to-west. The antenna feed attaches to the single tap I provided on the coil, about midway. Next time I'll add more taps to the coil to aid in tuning the antenna a bit better across the AM band. The full coil is paralleled with an air variable 365 uuf cap and attaches to the positive lead of the 1N34 germanium diode. The ear piece attaches to the diode negative lead and in parallel with the 47K detector resistor to ground. That's the rig!

Compared with a cylindrical coil, this set is hotter; I could hear five stations immediately, including Topeka (W1BW, 580), KC SPORTS (810) and of course the local, KLWM at 1320 on the dial.

Now back to the Morse! During my initial testing, I kept hearing brisk and loud TAT TAT TAT and TAT TAT TAT TAT, and TAT TAT TAT TAT TAT. It was perfectly sent, all at a steady 15 WPM. Wha???? I pulled off the earpiece and went upstairs to check on the source. Dang! I walked into the kitchen and the plumber was there repairing our gas range. Each time he turned the front burner on you could hear TAT TAT TAT TAT. Just like power line interference, the spark creates both RF and air tsunamis. So now my spouse sends lots of S, H, and 5 characters most days at 7 AM, sometimes noon, and usually around 6PM! 73, WØXI.

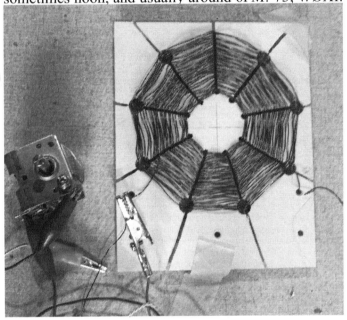

Picture 1

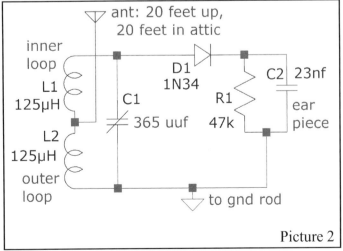

Picture 2

Back to Basics – Alternating Current
By Xtal Staff

In the January column of Back to Basics we introduced Ohm's Law as it relates to resistors. *Recall that the law describes the ratio of the voltage applied across a resistor to the current flowing through it as a constant called resistance.* As an example of the use of the law, we calculated the current resulting from the application of a battery wired across a resistor. While it was implicit, we didn't emphasize that our example used a constant voltage source, DC. In this article we describe alternating voltages and currents, generally called AC signals or sine waves. An understanding of AC sine waves will come in handy when we discuss capacitors and AC Ohm's Law in the next column.

We can describe the shape of a sine wave over time using a small weight hung on a spring, as noted in Figure 1. Let's make a couple of assumptions to begin with: the weight is small and when we pull it down a bit and release it the spring oscillates up and down but doesn't swing side to side. From experience we know what will happen. The weight will zoom back up, past its natural resting place and go about as far above as it was held below. If the spring isn't too stiff, the weight will cycle up and down for quite a while and eventually come to rest at its starting point. If we take a sequence of pictures while it is oscillating and plot the height of the weight over time we'll get the time trace shown in Figure 2. Note that the weight slows as it reaches its peak or lowest positions in each cycle but speeds up to a maximum as it crosses its original position going up or down. The result, plotted over time, is the shape we call the sine wave.

It is interesting that sine waves, sinusoids or phasors – whatever we like to call them – occur naturally in our world and beyond. For example, plot the latitude of the sun over a year and you'll see that it completes one cycle, swinging above the equator and then below. As we entered the 20th century electronic examples emerged. Consider the early power plants, where the voltage generated comes from a turbine, pushed round and round by water pressure. We can't see or hear the 60 cycle voltages and currents produced, but the shape of these signals over time is like that in Figure 2. And with the advent of electric spark gap transmitters at the

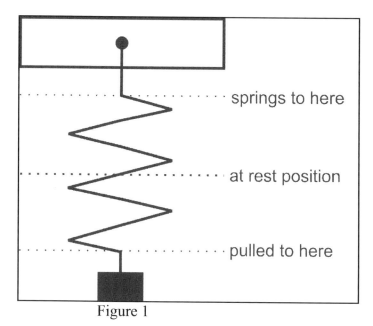

Figure 1

use a signal generator to apply an AC voltage to the same resistor with thermometer. Adjust the voltage level of the generator until the resistor temperature once again reaches that obtained by using the battery. The result must be that the effective voltage – also called the root-mean-squared (RMS) voltage – will be the same as the battery voltage. Most meters include an RMS scale. At the same time, if you examined the sine wave voltage with an oscilloscope, you would notice that the peak of the AC voltage is 1.414 times its effective or RMS average. We can write out these results as follows:

$$Veff = Vdc \text{ and } Vpeak = 1.414 * Veff; \text{ so,}$$

$$Veff = \frac{Vpeak}{1.414} \text{ which is the same as } \frac{Vpeak}{\sqrt{2}}.$$

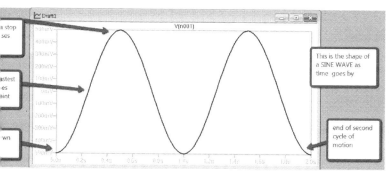

Figure 2

beginning of the 20th century, AC radio signals – called carriers - came into being. The common thing about all of these AC signal forms is that the shape of the signal if plotted out on paper or observed on the screen of an oscilloscope is the same!

When a DC voltage is applied across a resistor, we know how to calculate the current through it. We use Ohm's Law! But if the signal is wiggling up and down like our examples above, what do we use for <u>effective values</u> for the AC voltage and current? A hint lies in the following experiment.

Heating a Resistor With a DC and then an AC voltage.
Apply a 1.5V battery and a thermometer to a resistor and wait until the temperature of the resistor settles. Record the temperature. Then remove the battery and

You might wonder, "How could this be?" The answer lies in the fact that a sinusoidal current flowing through a resistor spends half of its time going in one direction and the other half going in the opposite direction. When the AC voltage applied to the resistor is positive the current will be positive and when the voltage swings negative the current will be negative too. Since the DC power supplied to the resistor is Vdc times Idc, the same formula must apply when the effective voltage is multiplied by the effective current. Thus

$$Veff \cdot Ieff = \frac{Vpeak}{\sqrt{2}} \cdot \frac{Ipeak}{\sqrt{2}}.$$

In our next back to basics segment, we'll introduce capacitors and develop an AC version of Ohm's law that will lead us to the concept of capacitive reactance, the effective impedance of capacitors at a given frequency.

Addendum
For you math-heads, here's the way a textbook might cover this subject. Another way to picture an alternating signal is to spin an arrow about its tail as shown in Figure 3. The amplitude of the AC signal at any instant of time is the height of the tip of the arrow above the horizontal line running through the center of the circle. For example, the solid arrow pointing upward at 30

degrees has an amplitude of a = 0.50. As the arrow rotates further counterclockwise it reaches a higher value with a height of b, and a maximum at c. As the arrow continues in time it reaches more than half way around the circle and the height of the point of the arrow is below the horizontal line at the center, thus drafting out negative values as noted in the graph of amplitude versus time. This is the shape of AC voltages and currents which we also called sinusoids.

A mathematical expression for an alternating voltage can be written as

$$v = V_m \sin(\omega t),$$

where $\omega = 2\pi f$ is the angular frequency,

f is the frequency in Hz,

t is time, and V_m is the peak value.

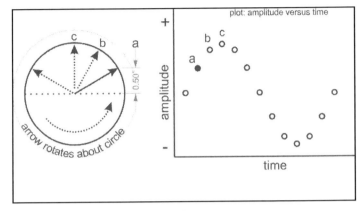

Figure 3

When a DC voltage is applied across a resistor, we know how to calculate the current through it. We'd use Ohm's Law! But how about the power delivered by an AC generator and consumed by the resistor? In general the instantaneous power received is equal to the voltage times the current; so, the instantaneous power can be deduced as follows:

$$power = v \bullet i = v \bullet \frac{v}{R} = \frac{v^2}{R}$$

and hence $v = \sqrt{power \bullet R}.$

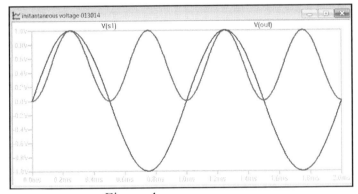

Figure 4

If the voltage applied is an AC signal then how are we to interpret the result? Let's try an example. Let's apply a 1 volt max, 1 kHz AC voltage to a 1 ohm resistor over two cycles. The results are plotted in Figure 4 at right. Clearly, the average voltage is

$$v(average) = \sqrt{(averagepower \bullet R)}$$

$$= \sqrt{0.5 * peakpower \bullet 1} = \sqrt{0.5},$$

so $v(average) = Vrms = 0.707.$

A 2-Tube Shortwave "Jenny"
by Dan Petersen, W7OIL

Sometimes it is refreshing to get away from the broadcast band with all their mindless crock-jock blather and go somewhere where the air is fresher – at least most of the time. There are numerous foreign and a sprinkling of domestic ones verbally parading their agenda to the world. One of the advantages of shortwave broadcasting is possible world-wide coverage with some really bodacious transmitter power. There is a big third-world audience that can hear shortwave broadcasts from other countries with very inexpensive receivers.

So what is a "Jenny"? Elmer Oldham knows the answer – "Jenny" is a slang term for a regenerative receiver. No receiver can combine such a simple circuitry with incredible sensitivity. For many years in the early 20th century the jenny reigned supreme in a ham-shack. The superheterodyne receiver was well developed by then, indeed it had been invented by Edwin Armstrong, inventor also of the regenerative detector! The bugger? The superhet ham set was hellishly expensive!

This column's project is a 2-tube regenerative receiver that uses relatively available parts. The variable capacitor and vernier drive are available from the XSS as is the crystal earphone. The vacuum tubes are available on the Internet, Peebles

Originals comes to mind as well as Antique Radio Supply. A bit of scrounging may be in order but that is a fine art you need to develop if you want to build homebrew projects. Ham radio fleamarkets are a great place to engage in what I call "spider-hunting"! The good stuff is usually under the table and full of dust, dead spiders, mummified mice and cool parts.

The concept of a regenerative detector is simple. A bit of the output is returned, in phase, to the tuned circuit and fed to the grid to be amplified further. Depending on the setting of the regeneration control the signal loops again and again. Do this enough and the detector tube (V1 in the schematic) will break into oscillation. This sword has two edges - oscillation is good if you want to listen

The Schematic

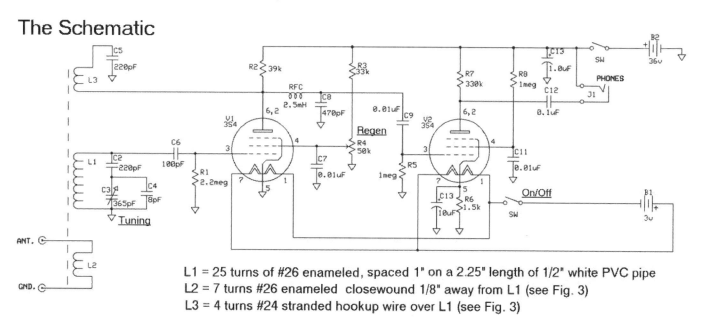

L1 = 25 turns of #26 enameled, spaced 1" on a 2.25" length of 1/2" white PVC pipe
L2 = 7 turns #26 enameled closewound 1/8" away from L1 (see Fig. 3)
L3 = 4 turns #24 stranded hookup wire over L1 (see Fig. 3)

to morse code but bad if you want to hear Radio Thundermug's talk show. So let's see how this set works. Signals are brought from the antenna and ground to L2. Inductively coupled to L1, the tuning coil, the signal is tuned by the L2,C2, C3, C4 network and passed to the grid of V1, the detector tube, via C6. V1 does its regeneration hocus-pocus with the audio & radio frequencies appearing on pin 6 and 2 of V1. Note pins 6 and 2 are connected together to the plate in a 3S4 tube. The radio frequency energy is stopped by the RFC (Radio Frequency Choke) while the audio passes through C9 to the grid of V2, the audio amplifier. This tube amplifies at full gain and presents the audio to the headphone jack (Phones).

Construction notes:

Figure 1 shows the layout of the receiver. I used my "Classy Chassis" approach (March, 2008 *Newsletter*), a wooden base with a Lexan chassis and front panel. I have laid out the components with the signal coming in at the left and the audio at the right, at least when looking at the front panel. The idea is to try to make the connections as short as possible. For the tuning coil I used a 2.25" long piece of white 1/2" PVC pipe. It looks dark in the photo because I put a strip of electrical tape along the length on the top and bottom. This helps secure the coil wire to the form and keep the coil windings from moving. The schematic notes that L1 is "space wound" this means the 25 turns need to be equally spaced over a one-inch length. L3 is the feedback winding. This is wound "closewound" meaning no gaps between turns. Figure 2 shows a detail of the coil. For those of you unfamiliar with PVC pipe, 1/2-inch pipe is NOT 1/2-inch in diameter! It's just under 7/8" outside diameter. Don't ask - I don't know either! You can see that L1 is spread out and you can see spaces between the turns. L3 is the closewound winding, as evidenced by the turns touching each other. L2 is called a "link" winding. This winding is preferable in the regenerative world for coupling to the antenna, rather than using a small capacitor. The reason is that, using a small capacitor adds the effects of the antenna to the tuned circuit. The effect may be small but at shortwave frequencies it can bugger things up. The use of a link also

seems, in my experience, to reduce hand capacitance and cure "dead spots" in the regeneration control.

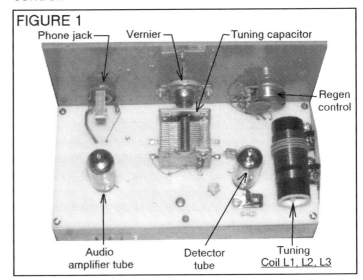

FIGURE 1

Phone jack — Vernier — Tuning capacitor

Regen control

Audio amplifier tube — Detector tube — Tuning Coil L1, L2, L3

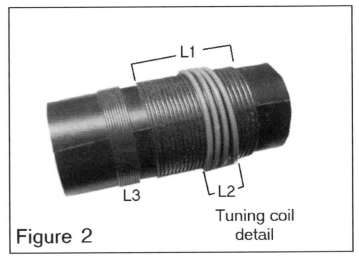

Figure 2

Tuning coil detail

The tubes are mounted on 7-pin miniature tube sockets and most of the support components are mounted on terminal strips. As seen in figure 1 a vernier drive turns the variable capacitor. These are more correctly called a "reduction drive" and this one provides a 6 to 1 ratio. Shortwave tuning *requires* some kind of slow-motion tuning!

You can see in the schematic that the regeneration control goes to the screen-grid of V1. This controls the DC voltage to the detector tube and as a result varies the amolification of the tube, In my estimation this is by far the best way to control regeneration. A DC voltage is being controlled while in a setup where the regeneration control is across the feedback coil there is RF going through the potentiometer. Messy. What you *do* need to be sure of is to place a bypass capacitor from the screen grid pin to ground *at the socket*. This goes for both tubes although with V2 you are running it at "full throttle".

The tuning dial I made from a piece of white Lexan. As seen in Figure 3 it is 3.25 inches in diameter and has an 11/32" diameter shaft hole and 2 mounting holes on either side for the 2-56 size screws for holding the dial to the vernier. Once I had the receiver up and running I calibrated the dial by putting the regenerative stage intentionally into oscillation and listening for it on my station receiver. Tune the station receiver (in this case an Icom R75) to a particular frequency, tune the Jenny until I heard it on the Icom and mark the frequency on the dial. Keep doing this over the entire range and there you have it.

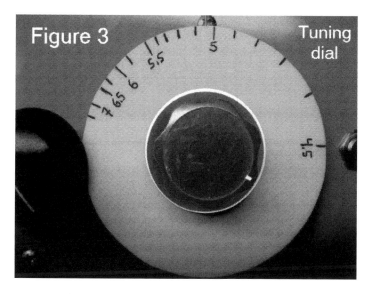

Figure 3 — Tuning dial

I wanted to point out the pitfalls of this type of receiver as well as the plaudits. One pitfall is that a "linear capacitance" variable capacitor is used. If you look carefully at the variable you can see that the shaft is at the center of the rotor. Another type of variable capacitor is the "frequency linear" capacitor. These have the shaft offset toward one side of the capacitor and the plates are arranged so that with a given inductor the frequency changes in a linear and not logarithmic manner. As seen on the dial for this receiver the higher frequencies are compressed closer than at the low end. So while a frequency linear capacitor would be better you "use what you got". If for some reason your regeneration doesn't regenerate try reversing the feedback leads.

For power I used two flashlight batteries for the filaments and five 9-volt batteries for the "B" battery. In this way you are working with "safe" voltages although you can get a bit of a tingle if you touch the "B" battery leads with damp fingers!

So what will you hear?

The shortwave bands are a fascinating place to explore. One reason I picked the frequency range I did was to be able to pick up the time station WWV at 5 megahertz and the 49 meter SWBC (Short Wave BroadCast) band around 6 megahertz. This is arguably the easiest band to find stations on and the propagation is fairly stable. What the Sun does to radio propagation is *entirely* another subject!

With this receiver I have no trouble receiving stations from the Deutsche Welle and the BBC as well as the big flamethrower, Radio Habana Cuba. WWV comes in fine during the evening. Long distance propagation tends to be much better at night. If you are into religion there are several fundamentalist stations ready to show you that your sinful life needs to be turned around so you can spend eternity plucking a harp and singing hosannas. You may find some "numbers stations", sending out endless "random" strings of numbers. This is "crypto" stuff that would take a computer the lifetime of the universe plus a week to decrypt. You can fiddle with the coil size a bit to drop the range into the 80 meter ham-band or the other way into the 40-meter band.

Experiment and have fun!

My Spider Web Crystal Radio Set..Revisited
By Phil Anderson, WØXI

In 1995 Ed Richley introduced his capacitive coupled crystal set in the Xtal Set Society newsletter. A decade later, Timoshenko Aslanides described his low-distortion set in a 2005 issue. And recently, we've reintroduced the Hi-Q spiral coil. It occurred to me that a combination of these techniques might make a nice AM receiver and indeed it does!

A block diagram combining these ideas is shown in Figure 1. A typical AM band antenna of 40 to 50 feet has a nominal resistance of roughly 200 ohms in series with a capacitance of about 300 pf. The resistance includes ground return losses. By adding a small adjustable tuning capacitor in series with the antenna the effective capacitance of the antenna is greatly reduced. The result is an antenna that barely loads the main tuned circuit, L1-C3, thus preserving its Q (1) (2). At the same time, if we use a very high-impedance detector, as Aslanides did, it doesn't affect the tuned circuit much either. The result is a set with more volume and better selectivity than most, particularly if we use a spiral coil wound with Litz wire (3). We chose a JFET follower biased below cutoff as our hi-impedance AM detector.

We were rewarded after wiring up the set; see the full schematic in Figure 2. With a 50 foot half vertical and half horizontal antenna and listening at 5PM on a clear winter day, we copied : WIBW 580 TOPEKA, KS;

KCSP "SPORTS" 610 KC,MO; WHB 810 KC MO; KMBZ 980 KC MO and KLWN 1320 our local flame thrower in LAWRENCE, KS. All five stations were strong and distortion of the audio was minimal. I guess some days we get lucky!

The infinite impedance detector, center of Figure 2, features a field effect transistor circuit configured as a source follower. The source resistor, R2, is enlarged to 22k to force operation of the JFET into its linear region below pinch-off. This arrangement does not affect detection but reduces distortion due to the non-linear operation of JFETS above pinch-off. The result is low-distortion audio. My 610 sports talk station sounds great now!

A full assembly of MY SPIDER is displayed in Figure 3. Left to right, we see the spider coil at the back, the JFET detector on its little 2 by 1.4 PCB and the antenna tuning cap and station tuning cap attached to the front panel. Except for the base, the coil form, chassis, and front panel are 1/8th inch pieces of white ABS plastic. Happy listening, Uncle Phil!

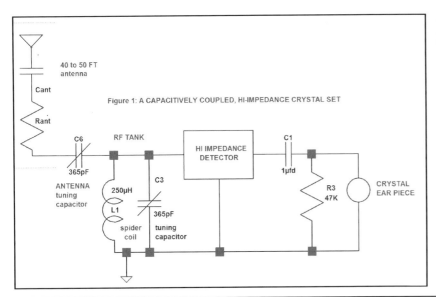

40 to 50 FT antenna

Figure 1: A CAPACITIVELY COUPLED, HI-IMPEDANCE CRYSTAL SET

Cant

Rant

C6 365pF
ANTENNA tuning capacitor

RF TANK

250µH
L1
spider coil

C3 365pF
tuning capacitor

HI IMPEDANCE DETECTOR

C1 1µfd

R3 47K

CRYSTAL EAR PIECE

References:

(1) Richley, Ed, "The Design of Unpowered AM Receivers Using Detectors Made from Rocks", 3 parts, The Xtal Set Society Newsletter, Vol 5, 1995.
(2) Anderson, Phil, "A Great Teacher: The Crystal Set": QEX Magazine, Sept/Oct 2008.
(3) Anderson, Phil, "The Spider Web (or Spiral) Coil, The Xtal Set Society Newsletter, Jan 2014.

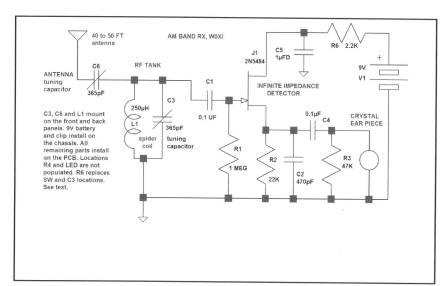

Figure 2

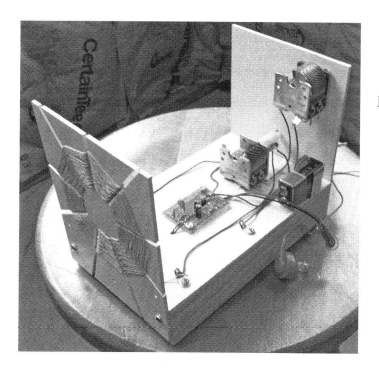

Figure 3

Ken Ladd's Three latest radios

I was inspired to build three crystal radios using novelty pencils as the coil form by a plan printed in the 1935 Modern Mechanix Radio Builders Manual. It was submitted by T.A. (Tom) Blanchard who went on to author other construction articles for radios, thermal generators, Vann Dgraff generators etc. For radio #1 I wound a travel tooth brush holder with as many turns of 24 AWG DCC copper wire as I could and slid it inside the chalk pencil and brought taps out to pin jacks. It is supported by plant stand parts, coat hanger wire and a plastic film canister cover. When I plugged the antenna, ground, 1N34 and 2000 ohm headphones into the appropriate jacks I was able to receive four or five local stations. I later added a variable capacitor for better tuning.

For radio #2 I used a thicker pencil that my daughter had pulled the eraser off of. It is also wound full of the same wire and tapped it. The radio is wired up as a Modern Radio Labs model 2 with two tuning capacitors and a broad and sharp tuning switch. I installed the 6H6 dual diode to look like the eraser and put 3vdc on the heater (six volts was too much) and can switch from the 1n34 to the tube

The panel is a cigar box lid sans the paper that my friend Del provided. The switch levers are NOS Modern Radio Labs and the switch points are unfired but deactivated 22 long rifle shell casings. The primers were hard to deactivate and are really loud when soldered on if they are still alive. The tuning knobs are vintage porcelain electric fence insulators with a coat hanger pointer. I used two MRL dial scales to accommodate the gear reduction variable capacitor. The only things I had to go out and buy were the PVC adapter and the tube. This happens to be the first tube type we experimented with in school in 1965. It receives local stronger stations ranging from KUOM (770) to KSTP (1500) and separates stations quite well due to the MRL 2 circuit.

Radio #3's panel is a cigar box sans the lid and

more unpredictable 22 shells. If I go this route again I think I will use copper plated rivets or spent small bore rifle cartridges like what I saw in an old book. Del gave me the large knobs to make tuning easier with the direct drive variable capacitors. I ran out of MRL switch levers and had to make one. The set uses four detectors. A 1N34, FO-215, NOS MRL fixed Carborundum, a NOS Philmore stand with a NOS Tip Top Special crystal from Del. I tried to use the novelty pencil point as a fox hole detector but it did not work. I cannot hear any difference in volume between the two diodes and they were comparable when tested o a Tektronix 576 curve tracer. Elmer liked to use heavier hook up wire which makes it hard to rotate the switch lever. To get around this I put a flat washer behind the panel followed by the terminal lug and another flat washer and a nylon center stop nut which works well. The nut is just tight enough to allow the screw to turn freely.

Getting the catwhisker to stay in place on the Philmore stand is usually a pain and you end up soldering it which I did not want to do. I tried to get it to latch onto the threads of a screw but that did not work. I removed the ball and the knob from the shaft and clamped it firmly in the vise with a small amount protruding above the vise jaws. I took a small hammer and tapped the end of the shaft to create a small ring of metal around the end of the shaft. I replaced the ball and flattened the knob end of the shaft in pressed the knob on in the vise. Then I simply pushed the catwhisher on the shaft and it securely locked onto the peened shaft.

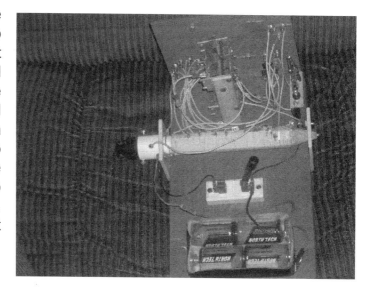

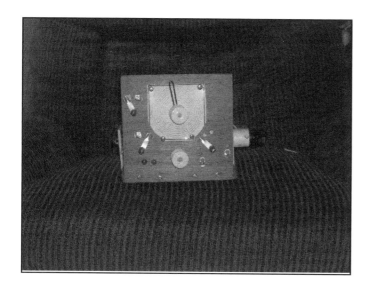

New Mechanical Panel Parts!
By Xtal Staff

From time to time, we've received emails from hobbyists/builders asking about behind the panel dials. Since there's been an uptick in inquiries of late, we decided to add some panel and dial hardware to our line of radio parts. Our newest items are displayed in Figure 1.

While just looking cool would be a reason for a dial setup, the primary reason often stated is the desire to display the change in position of the tuning capacitor rotor plates hidden behind a panel. In particular, when a reduction drive is added to the tuning shaft of a capacitor, a pointer knob on the front panel no longer displays the position of the capacitor rotor plates, since it turns six times faster than the capacitor blades. Most of us put up with this and simply look over the top of the panel when turning the knob to see where the capacitor plates are positioned. The situation can be remedied by cutting a slot in the front panel and attaching a dial position indicator of some sort to the primary shaft of the capacitor or a reduction drive.

We've designed the hardware shown in Figure 1 to accomplish these tasks. Let's introduce the new cast of parts and then we'll outline various ways of combining them. The round dial plate is 2.4 inches in diameter, 0.04 inches thick, has a 0.340 center hole and four mounting holes for 2-56 screws. The shaft dial coupler at upper right has a 0.87 inch diameter, 0.18 thickness, two 4-40 tapped holes in its side and a 0.250 center hole and two 2-56 mounting holes on its surface. The dial pointer, just below the coupler, is 1.075 inches long and is threaded 0.30 of an inch at one end. Finally, the grand prize, is the very nice looking 2 x 4 x 0.050 black anodized aluminum front panel, with laser labeled white graphics. The panel includes a circular "see through" cutout and four holes at the corners for mounting.

When adding a 6-1 reduction drive our goal is to display a dial plate or dial pointer via the cutout in the front panel that indicates the position of the capacitor plates. The back coupler of the reduction drive slips onto the shaft of the capacitor housed inside the chassis of the radio. The front of the coupler has two shafts: a knob shaft extending beyond the front panel and a

Figure 1

second shaft surrounding it and somewhat recessed, as noted in Figure 2. The reduction drive is secured to the chassis by our reduction drive L bracket set between the knob and the capacitor and secured to the chassis base.

Figure 2

The dial plate is slipped over the ¼-inch external shaft and secured to the secondary recessed shaft of the reduction drive using two 2-56 by 1/8th inch machine screws. A back view of the completed assembly is shown in Figure 3. Note the sequence of the assembly:

the rotor shaft of the capacitor is attached to the coupler at the back of the reduction drive; the L-bracket supports the drive above the chassis; the dial plate is secured to the larger recessed shaft at the front of the reduction drive and the knob shaft of the drive extends

Figure 3

out to accept a knob.

A front view of the completed assembly, including the dial panel is shown in Figure 4. We use a red stick-on dot on the dial plate to indicate the position of the top of the capacitor rotor plates. Some prefer to simply scribe a line with a knife on the surface of the round dial plate to indicate position. The position of the plates shown in Figure 3 matches up with the dot in Figure 4.

Figure 4

Figure 5 on the next page is an expanded view of the dial assembly.

Figure 6 displays the arrangement for adding a dial plate or dial pointer to the shaft of a regular 365 capacitor (that has no internal reduction drive built in). While a front panel label would indicate the position of the capacitor rotor plates in this arrangement, we added the shaft coupler to our bag of tricks so a radio using the regular 365 cap (without a reduction drive) could still make use of the recessed dial indicators.

The 365 is set back from the front panel and a ¼-inch dia. hollow 0.5 inch nylon shaft extender is added directly to the capacitor shaft. Following that a 0.25 by 1.5 inch nylon shaft is added that accommodates the shaft dial coupler. Then a shaft dial coupler is added at the junction of the two nylon shafts and a dial plate or threaded dial pointer is added to indicate capacitor's rotor position. Finishing up, a dial panel and knob are added to the front panel and shaft. The two screws shown in the 1 x ½ nylon shaft were added to secure it to the cap shaft and the 1.5 by ¼ inch nylon shaft extending out. We drilled and tapped the two holes to accommodate 4-40 screw to hold the shafts in place. Tap bits are readily available in hardware stores, such as ACE.

Figure 6

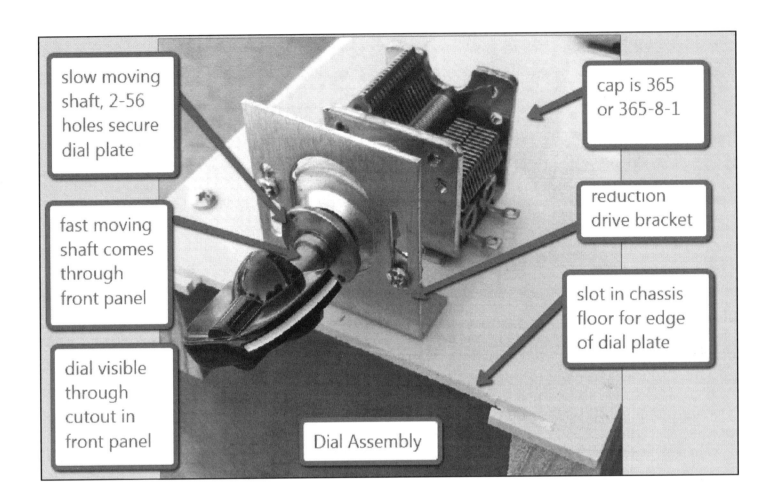

slow moving shaft, 2-56 holes secure dial plate

fast moving shaft comes through front panel

dial visible through cutout in front panel

Dial Assembly

cap is 365 or 365-8-1

reduction drive bracket

slot in chassis floor for edge of dial plate

Figure 5

Back to Basics, Coil and Capacitor Reactance, AC Ohm's Law
Xtal Staff

In the January issue we reviewed Ohm's Law as it relates to resistors. And in the March issue we discussed sine waves, often referred to as AC signals. In this piece we discuss AC Ohm's Law and inductive and capacitive reactance. It turns out that these tools/ideas allow us to determine the magnitude of an AC (sine wave) current flowing in a coil (inductor) or capacitor given the magnitude and frequency of an AC voltage applied across either of them.

The schematic symbols for a coil and capacitor are shown in Figure 1. We can see that the originators of these symbols drew them on paper to replicate what they'd look like in pictures. Can you see the windings of the coil in the figure? A capacitor is made of a bunch of stacked plates with some distance between each plate. Our drawing symbol shows the top and bottom plates with a lead coming out top and bottom. It is common to use the letter L for inductors and the letter C for capacitors. L1 then stands for coil 1 in the schematic and L2 would, of course, represent the next coil added to the schematic and so forth.

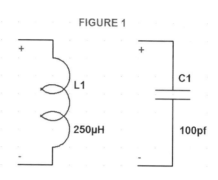

Sometimes the values of the coils and caps and other components will be included on a circuit drawing, in addition to being listed in a bill of material. The values shown in Figure 1 are typical for those found in a crystal radio designed for the AM broadcast band. The inductor is said to have an inductance of 250 micro-henrys (µH). The capacitor is said to have a capacitance of 100 pf (pronounced puff). In general, the inductance of coils is measured in Henrys or a fraction of a Henry and capacitor values are expressed in farads or a fraction of a farad.

Most coils used in radio equipment range in value from 0.001 to 0.000001 Henrys. To avoid writing all those zeroes, it is common practice to identify a 0.001 Henry coil as a milli-henry (mH) coil. So, a 10 mH coil is the same as a 0.01 Henry coil. Our coil in Figure 1 is valued at 250 uH, equivalent to .000250 Henrys.

Most capacitors used in radio equipment range in value from 0.000001 to 0.000000000001 farads, or one millionth (micro or µ) and one millionth-millionth (micro-micro or µµ) of a farad. Here, again, we wish to avoid writing all of the zeroes, so we substitute one micro-farad (µF) for a one millionth farad. In turn we use 1 uuF or 1 pf to represent the value of a one millionth-millionth farad capacitor. For capacitors used at radio frequencies, such as in the AM broadcast band, typical values range from 10 pf to 1000 pf. The capacitor shown in Figure 1 is a 100 pf cap.

Here are a couple of questions for you to drill. The answers are at the bottom of the article.
1. A 0.001 Henry coil is how many mH?
2. A 0.000250 Henry coil is how many uH?
3. A 0.33 Henry coil is how many mH?
4. A 1000 pf cap is how many farads?
5. A 100 pf cap is how many uF?
6. A 47 uF cap is how many farads?

Self-Inductance
In 1830 Joseph Henry discovered that current flowing in a coil has a property like mechanical momentum. Recall

that lifting a box is harder than simply carrying it. You seem to exert more energy in the lifting. A similar thing happens when one applies a battery voltage to a coil. The coil initially resists the flow of current from the battery; but, in time, the current builds up to a steady value, as noted in Figure 2. The circuit in this figure is used to simulate what happens when a 1 volt battery is attached to a 1 Henry coil that has an internal resistance of 1 ohm. Even though the resistor is shown external to the coil, the same thing would happen if the resistor were stuffed inside as part of the coil, which would be the real world case.

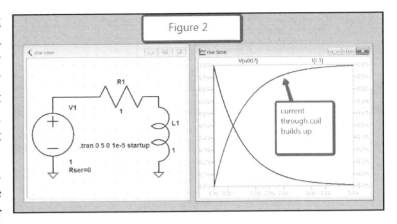

However, if an AC signal is applied to the coil, a curious thing happens. From the very start, the current following in the coil will be equal to the voltage applied times a proportionality factor made up of the inductance value and the frequency of the voltage. In this example, a small resistor was inserted inside the coil so that the current is limited. In the real world the coil would have its own small internal limiting resistor due to the wire coil. We display our result in Figure 3.

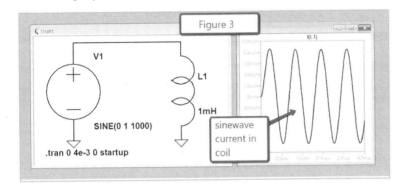

The resulting current can be calculated using the following equation; again the current will be proportional to:

As you may recall from Ohm's Law for resistors, the formula is exactly the same except for a coil we substitute ωL for R. Our result goes by a number of names: AC Ohm's Law for coils/inductors or we call ωL the inductive reactance. We can describe what happens in words as follows: when an AC voltage is applied to a coil, the resulting current will be equal to the voltage applied across the coil divided by the inductive reactance. So for AC circuits the resulting current is restricted by the frequency of the voltage source and the reactance of the coil. The higher the frequency of the voltage source the smaller the resulting current will be.

Magnetic Flux and Mutual Inductance
When an AC voltage is applied to a coil, we now know that an AC current will flow in the coil. This current in turn creates a magnetic field (flux) around the coil. So, if two coils are brought near each other the flux from each influences the other. In this way radio frequency energy can be transferred from one coil to another. We'll leave a detailed discussion of this for another back-to-basics presentation.

Capacitive Reactance

For the capacitor a similar equation can be written as follows:

$$v = \frac{i}{\omega C} = \frac{1}{\omega C} * i, \text{ where } \omega C \text{ is the capacitive reactance, C is the capacitance and } \omega = 2\pi f.$$

Again, as you may recall from Ohm's Law for resistors, the formula is exactly the same except for a capacitor you substitute 1/ωC for R. We can describe what happens in words as follows: when an AC current is applied to a capacitor, the resulting voltage will be equal to the current applied through the capacitor divided by the capacitive reactance. So for AC circuits, the resulting voltage is restricted by the frequency of the current source and the reactance of the capacitor. The higher the frequency of the source the lower the resulting voltage will be.

A Couple of Examples

So what kind of values will we get for inductive and capacitive reactance for L and C in the AM radio band? To see let's calculate the reactances of the coil and cap in Figure 1 at 1 Mhz (1000 kHz).

The inductive (coil) reactance will be equal to ωL, where f is 1 MHz and L is 250 uH; so

$$\omega L = 2\pi * 1MHz * 250uH = 2\pi * 1000000 * \frac{250}{1000000} = 2\pi * 250 = 1570.$$

So if 1 volt AC is applied to the coil, the current flowing in the coil will be 1/1570=0.636 ma.

The capacitive reactance will be ωC, where f is again 1 MHz and C is 100pf; so

$$\omega C = 2\pi fC = 2\pi * 1000000 * 100 pf = 2\pi * 1000000 * 100 / 1000000000000$$

$$\text{which when reduced becomes: } 2\pi * 100 / 1000000 = .000628 \text{ Ohms.}$$

So if a 1 ma current with a frequency of 1MHz is applied to the capacitor, the voltage across the capacitor will be about 1.592 volts.

Answers to questions 1 through 6:
[1]. 1 mH; [2]. 250 uH; [3]. 330 mH; [4]. 0.000000001 farads (or 0.001 uF); [5] 0.0001 uF; [6] 0.000047 farads.

The Tikker Detector Revisited –
The Beginning Of Radio Telegraphy
By Phil Anderson, WØXI

In the early days of radio telegraphy, designers initially applied existing land-line telegraph circuits to copy continuous radio frequency waves. (CW) For example, a coherer was used to detect RF dits and dahs and the resulting current would cause a holding relay to stay closed until the dit or dah was completed. A sounder was used to report a "click" at the beginning of the dit or dah and a "clack" at the end as the RF pulse ceased. Someone then thought of placing earphones across the holding relay in order to get more volume.

The next enhancement came when Poulsen (1) thought of using a chopper – also called an interrupter or tikker. He reasoned that to make un-damped radio frequency oscillations audible, one was "compelled to break up the oscillations in the headphones at an audio rate." With this addition, the dots and dashes sent could be heard more clearly, using a chop frequency of 300 to 1000 Hz. Note that this technique is not the same used in our modern day direct conversion receivers, wherein one mixes the RF signal with a local RF oscillator signal to create an audio beat note.

The schematic of the Poulsen Tikker is shown in Figure 1. The antenna and tuned circuit are shown at bottom left. C1 is used for RF tuning. The chopper consisted of a motor and timing wheel, with a constant connection from the tuned circuit to the flat surface of the wheel at B and an interrupting contact on the edge at A that feeds the phones. The dits and dahs arriving at the tuned circuit were literally chopped at an audio rate. The equipment delivered a reasonable audio tone after chopping, like those you'd hear today with a modern rig! Keep in mind that the frequency of carriers in those early days was typically from 40 to 100 kHz! In addition transmit power levels were quiet high as compared with low power (100W) and QRP power (5W) used for amateur CW transmissions today.

A MODERN DAY TIKKER

After revisiting this material on the Tikker, I decided to try building a modern version and testing it on the

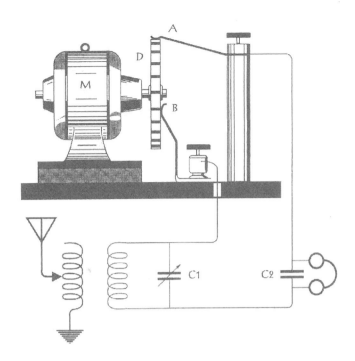

bench, using a signal generator and code key as the source. As with all electronic projects, I like to simulate them in software first and then build the hardware. This often saves overall project time and usually builds on a deeper understanding of results. Figure 2 shows a wave/signal result and associated pseudo-schematic.

The signal generator, V1, is shown at bottom left in the schematic. I multiplied the output of the generator with a 500 Hz square wave (0 to 1 VPP) that lasted for 5 ms and ran the simulation for 10 ms, thus simulating the action of the chopper wheel. The resulting multiplication is reported by block B1, a behavioral source; and the result is shown as V(out-b1) in the software graph at the top of the figure. Clearly one sees the results of chopping the RF signal five times and then leaving it open. Finally, I added a JFET detector with the output at the source lead. Hi-Z phones were attached in place of R1. The detector, of course, presents the envelope of the RF as audio. We'll discuss why I added this in a bit.

The schematic for my actual wired circuit and a picture of the bench build are shown in Figures 3 and 4. Let's take a walk through the schematic first. A BK Precision 4017B is shown at left and labeled "RF." The chopper features a CD4066BCN IC switch and 500 Hz, 3-gate 74HC14 inverter oscillator (2). The JFET detector and an LM386 audio amplifier complete the circuit. Let's focus on the switch. Plus and minus supplies or bias-

---

ing of the input and output signals must be supplied to switch AC signals. I didn't want to mess with a -5V supply so I AC-coupled and biased the input and output at pins 1 and 2. The audio square wave drives the clock input at pin 13 with a 0 to 5VP signal. The square wave can be implemented in a number of ways, using three 74HC14 inverts, using a 555 timer, a PIC, and so on.

How does the output sound? Actually it sounds pretty good. With the generator set for 100 mvpp and the local oscillator set at 500 Hz, I varied the frequency and mvpp of the RF signal and keyed in a few CQs for a variety of frequencies. For the circuit of Figure 3 – with the output taken from the detector - the code sounds fine with RF carriers of 2 MHz, 200 kHz, even 20 kHz. With a carrier at 2 kHz we get a buzzing sound. This is as expected when the input carrier and audio oscillator frequencies are too close together. With the output of

the chopper taken directly to the LM386 audio amp, i.e. bypassing the JFET detector and receiving a waveform like that in Figure 2, the code sounds good with a carrier of 2 MHz but the volume is down some. In addition, the code is grainy sounding below 200 kHz, again with less volume.

Now recall that the Tikker in Figure 1 had no detector added ahead of the phones. I had wondered what that would sound like. Now we know. It works but not as well as when a detector is added.

Next step? I hope to find the time to add a tuned circuit front end and see if I can copy any local CW traffic across town on 40 meters. "Look Mom! No local RF oscillator!" Or perhaps I should have said, "Look Grandma! No local RF oscillator!"

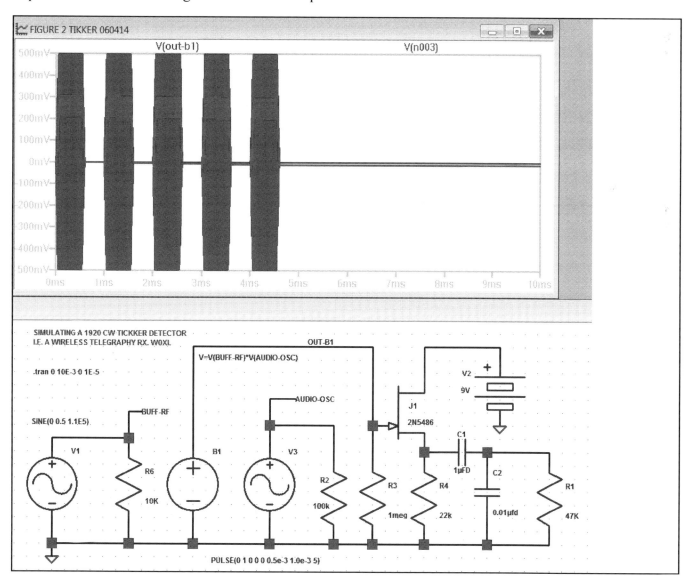

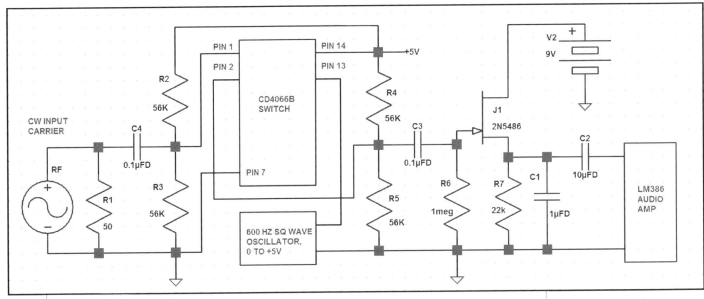

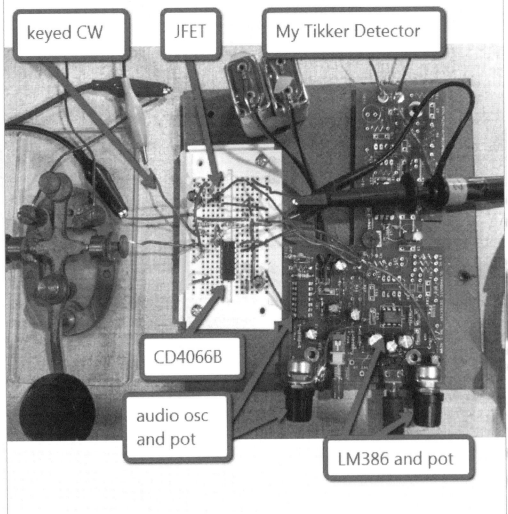

REFERENCES

(1) Bucher, Elmer, Practical Wireless Telegraphy, Part XV, page 278, 1917.
(2) Google the CD4066BCN IC and the 74HC14 invertor for pin outs and app notes. Vendors carry these parts today.

Modifying the JFET Radio
by Chip Olheiser

I bought this kit from you several months ago and put it together. It didn't perform well at all. I called you 2 times, we discussed it and then I ran the tests you suggested that day on JFET circuit board and tests passed. Something else must be wrong with the set. I shelved the project for later investigation.

When I had time to investigate, I did the following:

working directly from your schematic,
1. rewired antenna connections
2. rewired coil wiring
3. rewired capacitor wiring
4. all leads to / from circuit board
5. moved thumb pot / changed with a panel mount wire wound 100k pot

I now get plenty of loud audio. I am plugging the set headphone output into my station master mixer audio panel, and yes, I get very much more audio gain, but that's just fine with me.

My mixer system has dual 8 channel summing junctions to unity gain lm386 audio circuits. These outputs are then sent to rf hardened Bose stereo receiver aux input which in turn drives the Bose set internal left / right amplifiers and left / right speakers. I have operator select for mono or stereo for each channel. I use the Bose amplifiers

and speakers as a master station, 16 channel input, mono or stereo output, audio mixer.

One of these mono inputs is connected to the JFET set output.

JFET Set Modifications
I made two modifications/ improvements to the JFET set from stock design/ build:

1. moved "thumb pot" on circuit board, to front panel of set using 100k wire wound pot so operator can now optimize the bias on the JFET from the front panel.
2. added two test points on rear chassis for connecting oscilloscope across audio out (headphone jack output).

The set works very well with my cha250b ham vertical antenna and has plenty of volume. I am able to pick up stations several hundred miles away at night.

With taps set as shown in the pictures, I get the following performance:

1. tuning range 507 khz to 2495 khz
2. FET thumb pot (now on front panel) adjust range about 200 mv pp or more
3. mds (rough measure at 1 mhz), approx –40 dbm, using my spectrum analyzer, hp 8494a, 8496a, precision step attenuators

The set is working very well.

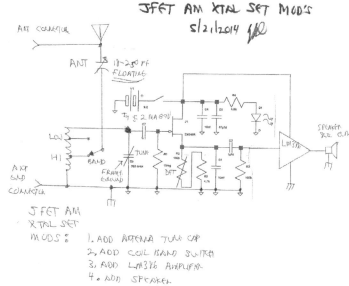

More Modifications To My JFET XTAL Set.

1. Add antenna tune trimmer capacitor

2. Add coil band switch

3. Add lm386 audio amplifier

4. Add speaker

See schematic and pictures.

To Infinity and . . . Turn Left at the Corner.
by Dan Petersen - W7ØIL

Infinity: An abstract concept involving numbers, most used in mathematics and physics. Infinity is represented by the symbol "∞" which looks like an "8" that is too lazy to get up. Infinity is like tomorrow. It is in the future but never arrives. In arithmetic, oh excuse me... it's now called "number theory" - as I was saying, in arithmetic ∞+1=∞, ∞-1=∞, ∞*1=∞, but 1/∞="infinitesmal". Infinitesmal can also be thought of as "REALLY itty-bitty. So close to zero but still infinitely far away! Confused? Good - we're getting there. There are concepts that are *practically* infinite; The number of stars in the universe. the number of bacteria on the Earth. the number of government employees, the list goes on. Practically infinitesmal includes things smaller than a sub-atomic particle and the amount of compassion in an IRS agents heart. Included in the list of "practically infinite" is the "Infinite Impedance Detector". This device may not be truly infinite in impedance, but for all practical purposes it is.

Why do you need an infinite impedance detector? To answer this question we need to look at the venerable crystal radio. My reader knows that a crystal radio is not much more than a tuned circuit and a detector. Connect antenna, ground and phones and voila!, crock jocks abound! If we look at the tuned circuit it boils down to an inductor (coil) and a capacitor connected in parallel. They form what is called a "resonant circuit". Both have a property that is called "reactance". At a certain frequency, a capacitor has a "capacitive reactance", given as XC. This value is dependent on the frequency and the capacity value. For a set capacity the reactance value in ohms will decrease as the frequency increases. The opposite holds true for "inductive reactance" for a coil. An increase in frequency on a coil will result in an increase in "inductive reactance". Another way engineers like to astound the marks is to use "j" in a complex impedance formula. The lower case "j" is an intangible expression that has little meaning unless it has a polarity. So a complex impedance can be expressed as 50+j50=Z. The

"plus" indicates that the value is inductive while a "-j" indicates a capacitive value. The actual reactance value cannot be measured with a meter but can be calculated. I am not writing this though for a mathematical dissertation - I want to get back to something tangible. Looking at Figure 1, you can see that at one point, the reactances cross. That happens at only one place and that is called "resonance". The reactances will cancel out!

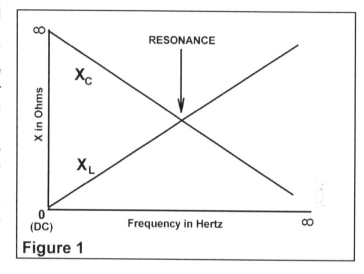

Figure 1

A tuned circuit all by its onesey is usually a pretty sharp character. It will pass one frequency while blocking all others. This is what is referred to as "Q". This is also "in theory". Placing a load like a resistor will cause the "Q" to decrease. This causes the tuned circuit to pass more frequencies. The first crystal set I built was connected to a low impedance earphone, the kind you'd find with a transistor radio in those days. At about eight ohms impedance it loaded the tuned circuit to the point that I could hear only one station, faintly, and tuning only made it go up and down a bit in volume. A high impedance (~2000 ohms) headphone would have improved the tuning and the volume. So the lesson is this: put as light a load as you can on the tuned circuit.

What a load of...resistance?

So what to do about "Q"? One way to decrease the load on the tuned circuit is as I mentioned, use high-impedance headphones. Good but 2000 ohms still loads the tuned circuit. Art Bell will have competition from adjacent stations. You can put the detector part-way down the coil and it will decrease the loading and increase selectivity. It will also decrease the volume of the output. You can use a crystal earphone and then you can place 47 thousand ohms of resistance in parallel with it. The resistor is necessary because the crystal earphone looks electrically like a capacitor and will charge up from the direct current component of the detector output and work poorly. That amount of resistance is STILL a long way below infinity.

To Infinity...

Many years ago, when the vacuum tube was king there developed a device called the "infinite-impedance" detector. Simply enough it was a triode tube that was cathode biased with a large value resistor and the grid connected directly to the tuned circuit. There was no grid current to speak of. With an RF voltage impressed on the grid with no current flow the effective input impedance was...infinite! With this circuit your tuned circuit "Q" was not (in theory) affected. There's that "in theory" stuff again! There are other considerations such as stray inductances and other residual fancy electronic words. These to a smaller extent affect the overall operation. For the most part the effect is small.

The bipolar transistor was supposed to inherit the crown from the vacuum tube but the best it could do was be "Prince Regent" to the venerable glass king. The bipolar transistor must have some current flow through the base to operate so the concept of infinite impedance goes out the window. Around 1958 the "field-effect" transistor was developed. With the FET there was practically no current flow so the input impedance went into the megohm region. With the IGFET (Insulated Gate

FET) the impedance went into the gigohm region and above. Not infinity but it might as well be.

Building an Infinite-impedance Detector

The Xtal Set Society's Prince Consort, Philip of Kansas, AKA Phil Anderson, WØXI, Has developed an infinite-impedance detector that is available at modest cost from the XSS. My curiosity finally won out and I ordered on of his detectors. A few days later a nicely packed package arrived via USPS and I eagerly opened it. My dreams were crushed - there was NO CANDY MINT in the box! Some compassionate soul in the vast shipping department of the XSS used to include a mint with each order. I guess times change (sigh). The kit was well packed with all the parts necessary, a nicely marked well made circuit board, a battery clip and a crystal earphone. The kit also included

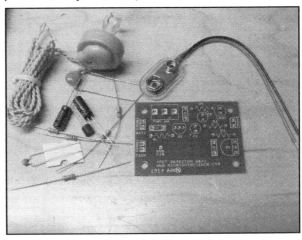

a nicely written set of step-by-step instructions and theory of operation.

I followed the instructions and found almost nothing to gripe about. The only thing is to read each step CAREFULLY. The only addition to the instructions I would include would be to include the resistor color bands for those who have a bit of trouble with the resistor color code. Hence the 1-megohm resistor would have "brown-black-green-gold" included with the value. If your resistor starts with a gold band turn the resistor around!

You want to use a soldering iron with a MAXIMUM of 25 watts. Also if you have "Old Fogey" eyes like I have, a magnifier of some sort is very handy. The capacitor markings are hard to see. Construction, while taking my time, took about 30 minutes. The "pads" where the parts leads go through the board are quite small and do not require a lot of solder. The board was designed for more than one application so follow the directions!

I soldered the crystal earphone into its place and soldered a couple of short wires to the input. First I checked the set to make sure it worked OK with my "Less than RMS Titanic" antenna. Yup. The set works pretty good. With the 1N34 diode on the coil tap and my 4500 ohm magnetic headphones the stations were separated nicely. I then placed the diode on the top end of the coil and several stations blasted through at the same time - a classic case of tuned circuit loading! I connected the crystal earphone to the diode detector, using the

4500 ohm 'phones as a load and listened. The sound was OK but "tinny" sounding, usual with crystal earphones.

It's Aliiiive!

I connected the infinite impedance detector to a 9-volt battery while measuring the current draw. The detector pulls a miniscule 110 MICRO-amperes. It would take a LONG time to drain the battery. I used clip-leads to connect to the top of the tuned circuit and listened through the crystal earphone. Whoa! What a difference! The audio quality was much improved and the selectivity was VERY good. This reflects the very high impedance of the FET detector. While it could be said it is not strictly infinite in impedance it might as well be!

I then tried it with the 4500 ohm magnetic headphones and was very pleased with the volume and the audio quality. The infinite impedance detector is arguably a "unity-gain" amplifier also known as a "source-follower" amplifier. The voltage gain is near a gain of 1 but it does show current gain.

I think Phil's infinite impedance detector is an interesting addition to your crystal radio experimentations. Perhaps it would be useful in a Shortwave crystal set design. At shortwave frequencies the "Q" of a tuned circuit must be as high as possible. I plan to do some more detailed examinations of this detector such as linearity tests as the audio quality is quite good.

Keep expeerimenting!

Back To Basics: Coils

By J. K. Fenton

A bare bones crystal set consists of an antenna, coil, tuning capacitor, detector, crystal ear piece and a resistor. Figure 1 displays several useful wiring arrangements of these parts. The connection of the diode, resistor and capacitor are the same for each circuit. Assuming the use of the ubiquitous 1N34 diode, crystal ear piece and 47K resistor, there isn't much one can do to optimize performance of a set further for these parts. Increased volume and selective tuning are obtained by optimizing the quality and arrangement of the coil with the antenna and tuning capacitor. An air variable tuning capacitor is normally used and what you see is what you get; that is, you can't improve it. Hence, to improve these basic sets, you must optimize the quality of the coil and the way it is attached to the circuit as a whole.

In general these sets are tuned – that is, a station is selected – by adjusting the resonant frequency of the coil and

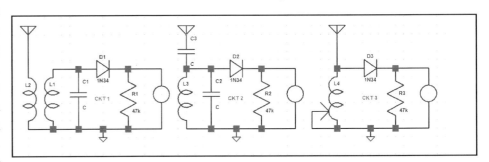

tuning capacitor pair. The coil has a single value – called its inductance; so, the pair must be tuned using the variable capacitor (circuits 1 and 2). In the case of circuit (3) the length of the coil is adjusted by a tap to tune the set, since the antenna serves as a quasi-constant capacitor. We'll cover antenna circuits at another time.

Coils have several parameters and values. The obvious parameters are those that you can see: the total length, type and diameter of the wire and the number of turns. In addition, the coil may be wound on a form of some sort, such as a piece of PVC pipe, a cigar box or a flat plastic sheet. Alternatively the coil can be wound/woven on a special form, glued and then removed, such as a basket-weave coil. With all of these, the inductance of these coils of different shapes could be the same if desired. For example, you could have a cylindrical coil or spiral coil with the same inductance. In general the inductance of a cylindrical coil is proportional to its radius, length, and number of turns. In formula form the inductance in micro-henrys (uH) is equal to

$$L(uH) = \frac{r^2 N^2}{10l + 9r}, \text{ where r} = \text{radius (inches)}, l = length \text{ (inches)} and \text{ N the no of turns.}$$

For the spiral or spider coil (wound on a flat surface and spiraling outward like a pancake) the formula is similar,

$$L(uH) = \frac{(rN)^2}{8r + 11wN}, \text{ where r is the mean radious (inches), w is wire dia (inches), and N is no. of turns.}$$

Note that the inductance formulas are similar. In general the inductance of a coil is proportional to the square of the radius times the square of the turns divided by a radius and width-like factor. Either coil could have a higher quality than the other. Let's define this "quality factor." In formula form the quality factor can be defined in several ways:

$$Q = \frac{f_o}{BW} = \frac{\omega_o L}{r}, \text{ where } f_o \text{ is the resonant frequency of the LC circuit,}$$

BW is the effective bandwidth, ω is the radian frequency, L is the inductance and r is the "ac" resistance of the coil wire.

The first formula says in effect that the quality of the LC circuit, Q, is highest when the peak frequency of the resonant circuit divided by the bandwidth of the circuit is highest. So we can interrupt this as high Q means high quality because the circuit tunes sharply (gives us a narrow filter). The second expression says that the Q is equal to the inductive reactance (ωL) of the coil divided by the resistance (r) of the coil wire. So you want sharp tuning and low resistance in your crystal set coils in order to have selectivity and improved sensitivity.

How does the sensitivity plan in? When the resistance is low, the voltage in your LC circuit can grow to a larger value than before. In this case there is more voltage on the tuned circuit to overcome the threshold of that ole pesky 1N34 detector diode.

Finally, there are two more hidden factors that reduce coil Q: the skin and proximity effects. The higher one goes in frequency the more resistive the wire becomes. What happens is the current in the wire is pushed outward toward the wire surface; hence, there is less effective copper for the RF current to flow in and that "r" in the Q formula reduces the Q. That's why Litz wire (many fine strands) are used in place of a larger single conductor; this provides more effective copper for the current to flow in and hence better Q! Finally, the closer windings are wound together, the more they insist on resisting the RF current flow in each other; this is the proximity effect. Fortunately, if you simply space adjacent turns at least one turn diameter apart (an air gap if you will), this effect is reduced to a good extent.

So, who said crystal sets are simple? Ask your critic to explain the geometric, skin, and proximity effects! Bet he or she cannot!

The society has a coil calculator on its website. Go to www.midnightscience.com/formulas to see it.

The Crystals of "Crystal Radio"

BY HP Friedrichs, AC7ZL

"Crystal Radio." The very term for this technology contains, embedded within it, reference to the iconic material responsible for extracting intelligence from the waves in the aether—the detector crystal. Sadly, it seems that most contemporary crystal set builders interpret this word to mean a factory-made 1N34 germanium diode. Even among adventuresome builders, those who might craft their own crystal cups and cat's whisker mechanisms, rarely is attention paid to natural detector materials outside of galena.

In truth, there is a wide variety of metallic minerals that exhibit useful electrical properties, and in the early days of radio many of them were pressed into service.

What is a crystal detector? In essence, it is a primitive semiconductor, not unlike the silicon or germanium-based diodes found in modern electronics, except that they are usually comprised of naturally-occurring—as opposed to human-engineered—materials. Detector behavior emerges when pairs of materials, two different types of crystal for example, or a crystal and a wire probe, are brought into intimate contact. A complete detector includes not only the raw materials just mentioned, but some kind of adjustable mechanical contrivance used to position and hold the semi-conducting materials against one another.

So which naturally-occurring materials make for a good detector? Table 1 contains a list of possible candidates that I've assembled. The list is by no means exhaustive, but it does draw from multiple sources including the October 1925 edition of J.F. Corrigan's *Crystal Experimenter's Handbook*, Ralph Stranger's 1928 work *Wireless The Modern Magic Carpet*, Alfred Morgan's 1913 *Wireless Telegraph Construction for Amateurs*, Chris Pellant's 1992 *Rocks and Minerals*, and assorted books and materials from my personal library.

The first column in the table contains the names of various mineral types. Note that some minerals are known by more than one name, and if I could determine that, I included references to both. I did not acknowledge period references to "inserite," "tserine," or "iserine" because, frankly, I could find no mention of them in any of the more modern books that I have. As I am not a geologist, I'll accept fault for their exclusion. Maybe these particular names are no longer in vogue or the substances in question are now known by different, newer names.

Some substances were flagged by Corrigan as being commercially successful detector materials. These I've signified in the table with a bold font.

The next three columns tell us something about the chemical composition of each mineral. Column two provides a chemical name, column three specifies a chemical formula, and column four classifies the compound. In extracting data from period sources I noticed that some of the chemical information was in minor disagreement with more modern sources. In those cases, I defaulted to the more recent data.

Column five is of particular interest, because it says something about what combinations of materials will result in useful detectors. This information was taken primarily from Corrigan.

Column six reflects specific references to minerals made by Corrigan in his *Crystal Experimenter's Handbook*, mentioned earlier. An "X" appears in the row of any mineral described by that book. Column seven reflects the recommendations of a Dr. D.H. Eccles who is quoted in Stranger's *Magic Carpet*. Column eight represents the recommendations of Japanese scientist Wichi Torricata whose comments were published in the September 16, 1910 edition of *Electrician*. The *Electrician* piece, incidentally, is also cited in Stranger's book. Column nine represents references in Alfred Morgan's work.

It comes as no surprise that galena is on the list, and is endorsed by four authors. Because my own experience with galena detectors involves crystals probed with the classic wire "cat's whisker," it was interesting to discover that a galena detector can also be built with galena-on-galena, silicon-on-galena, and graphite-on-galena. In the latter case, I can envision probing the galena crystal with a soft (low clay content) #1, #2 or B-grade pencil lead.

My favorite whisker material for galena is phosphor bronze wire. As a guitar player, I enjoy a ready supply of phosphor bronze wire in the form of used acoustic guitar strings. In guitar strings, the bronze wire is wound around a core of steel music wire to thicken the string and reduce its pitch, generally the low "E," "A," and "D" strings. Extraction of the bronze wire involves no more than unwrapping a segment of guitar string to remove whatever length of bronze wire is needed.

Speaking of pencil leads, any crystal radio builder worth his salt has heard of the so-called "foxhole" radio. First described in the July 1944 issue of QST magazine, the foxhole radio was a primitive crystal receiver devised by clever soldiers stationed on the Anzio beachhead. Their detector was comprised of a blued razor blade probed by a piece of pencil lead. Chemically speaking, the bluing is a form of magnetite and pencil lead is, of course, predominantly graphite. Both of these materials are represented in Table 1.

Also to be expected, iron pyrites appear in the table. Iron pyrite, or "fool's gold" is a readily-available and cheap mineral to purchase and play with. I have found that while not all samples make effective detectors,

most do. My favorite configuration involves the pyrite crystal probed with a steel wire whisker. Music wire with its high carbon content is nice and springy, and can also be harvested from guitar strings (I suggest the 0.008-0.010-inch high "E" strings). I provide detailed plans for a pyrite detector in Chapter 11 of my book, *The Voice of the Crystal*.

Another detector material that I have some experience with, which appears in Table 1, is cuprous oxide. I've written extensively on experiments with this substance in my book *Instruments of Amplification*, and my article "Fun With Homebrew Cuprous Oxide Diodes" which appeared in the January 2010 issue of the *Xtal Set Society Newsletter*. The mineral form of cuprous oxide is called cuprite. In the case of my experiments, the oxide I used was created artificially on the surface of carefully-prepared samples of copper metal.

Table 1 suggests tellurium and antimony as suitable contacts for use with cuprite. Homegrown cuprous oxide films, however, are fragile and are subject to unintentional scratches or penetration. Thus, my favorite probe material for cuprous oxide is metallic lead or solder. Unlike harder metals like bronze or steel, lead is soft and compliant. As well, I've experimented with tiny beads of indium and even dots of silver-bearing ink. All work well as contact materials. Though I haven't tried it, graphite might be worth a look.

Given my own success with copper oxides, I find chalcocite, or copper sulfide, an intriguing variation. I've never played with chalcocite, but Corrigan's handbook describes a technique for making your own copper sulfide detector.

One must carefully melt a small quantity of sulfur until it's fully liquefied. The end of a copper rod, previously cleaned and polished to a bright shine with emery paper, is immersed in the liquid for several minutes, and then withdrawn. Finally, the coated end of the rod is ignited, and any free sulfur that remains is allowed to burn off. Corrigan reports that the coating thus formed works well in contact with zincite, or even when probed by the usual cat's whisker. The author does not mention what I feel I must: Such preparations will surely result in the production of toxic fumes, so experiments like this should be conducted outdoors, and then only while wearing suitable protective gear like leather gloves and safety glasses.

If one mineral can be said to dominate Table 1, that would be zincite. Zincite, it seems, will produce a useful detector junction with just about everything else. Zincite in contact with a copper pyrite crystals form the basis of G.W. Pickard's legendary "Perikon" detector.

Zincite has the additional property that, if stimulated properly, it can be induced to both amplify and to oscillate-- the very properties that make modern transistors so useful. It is a pity that much of the interest in crystal oscillators vanished when practical vacuum tubes first appeared. However, contemporary experimenters like Nyle Steiner have rediscovered and written about this phenomenon.

Given the random processes responsible for natural crystal formation, the specific chemical content of a given mineral type is subject to variability imposed by the whims of nature and chance. For example, if foreign substances are present when minerals are being formed, those compounds may be integrated into the emerging crystals, thus modifying their physical properties. In crystal radio terms, this can result in the non-responsive or "dead" detector mineral that early radio enthusiasts occasionally grumbled about. However, sometimes the type and concentration of the adulterants is such that they actually enhance the signal-detecting properties of the crystal. Two examples of this readily come to mind.

Galena, chemically speaking, is a lead sulfide. However, my readings suggest that the best galena for crystal radio detectors is not pure, but a type which contains trace amounts of silver. This latter type of galena, called argentiferous galena, is said to produce superior detectors, both in sensitivity and stability.

Another example is zincite. Zincite is a simple oxide of the metal zinc. Pure synthetic zincite crystals are typically clear and colorless, but from what I've gathered, the zincite with the most desirable radio properties is red. This red color manifests itself in the zincite crystals because they've been naturally tainted with manganese and iron.

Incidentally, modern semiconductor manufacturers make routine use of contaminants in their products, albeit in an intentional and carefully-controlled manner. The purpose of this is to beneficially alter the electrical properties of the materials from which transistors and integrated circuits are made. The industry calls this practice doping.

A complete list of naturally-occurring detector materials would far exceed the contents of Table 1. However, when it comes time to apply these materials to an actual radio receiver, certain practical considerations immediately shrink the size of any pool of candidates.

For example, some minerals are comparatively rare or exhibit detrimental chemical properties. Despite Torricata's endorsement, syvanite is a good example of both. It is a fairly rare crystal which tends to makes it very pricey. Then, some instances of sylvanite are actually photosensitive and will tarnish upon exposure to light.

An ideal detector should be easy to adjust and set into action. Once set, the detector should remain functional over a useful interval of time. Yet, success with many natural detector materials depends upon the pressure with which the crystals are probed. Some require robust pressure between crystals or the crystal and its whisker. Other detector materials will function with the slightest touch. Some are so sensitive to mechanical shock that it's difficult to get them properly adjusted, and once so, a hard stare is sufficient to knock them out of whack. Despite otherwise useful properties, such unstable materials will result in a detector that is more trouble than it's worth.

It is best if a detector is "sensitive." Sensitivity is a consequence of the voltage that must be applied to the crystal in order to get it to conduct, and the rate at which current through the crystal rises with further increases in applied signal. Why is this important? Because if we attempt to detect a radio signal whose amplitude lies below the threshold of conduction for the detector, the detector will remain in an "off" condition and the signal will not be heard.

Let's talk about carborundum in the context of these last few paragraphs. Carborundum is a synthetic industrial abrasive. It doesn't have to be mined, and there is no shortage of it because it's easy to make. Consequently, carborundum is relatively easy to obtain and its price is reasonable.

Carborundum is normally probed with steel, another common material. Carborundum likes firm contact between itself and the steel probe, which lends itself to the construction of mechanically stable detectors. Once adjusted, a carborundum detector tends to stay properly adjusted for a long time.

Regrettably, carborundum is not a very radio-sensitive material. Whereas a galena detector or a germanium diode like the 1N34 will begin conducting signals as small as a few tenths of a volt in amplitude, a carborundum detector will not function properly until the applied signal reaches a volt or more—a tenfold reduction in comparative sensitivity—which renders it useless for weak-signal work. Figure 1 is a graph adapted from Bucher showing the response curve for a typical carborundum crystal. Given this apparent lack of sensitivity, why is carborundum bolded in Table 1, signifying it as a commercially successful detector material?

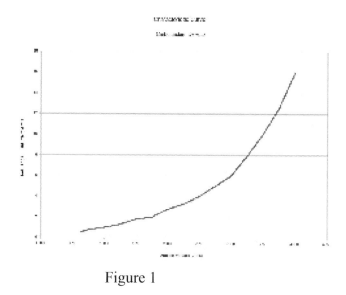

Figure 1

It turns out that carborundum's problems can be mitigated through the careful application of what is called a "bias voltage." The idea is to use a small battery to apply an electrical potential on the detector that is almost, but not quite, sufficient to force it into conduction. Operating the crystal in this manner means that a radio signal superimposed on the bias, even a very

tiny signal, will then be sufficient to trip the crystal into conduction. It should be understood that the same technique can be applied to other detectors to varying degrees of advantage.

Figure 2 depicts a simple crystal receiver with an option to bias its detector. The circuit was adopted from the Marconi Model 107A Tuner.

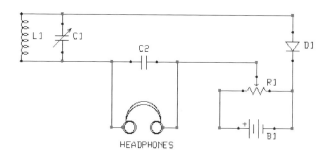

Figure 2

The biasing circuitry consists of nothing more than a couple of dry cells in series (B1) and a potentiometer (variable resistor, R1). When the potentiometer is at its lowest setting (to the far right), battery current flows through the potentiometer only. No potential is applied to the detector (D1). As the potentiometer is advanced to the left, however, an increasing voltage will be applied to the detector through a circuit completed by the headphones and tuning coil (L1). Figures 3, 4, and 5 depict minor variation on this basic idea.

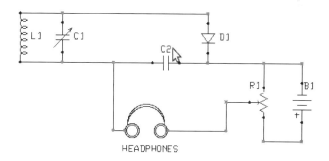

Figure 3

What is the correct point of adjustment? That depends upon the detector materials in use and is best determined through trial and error. Too much bias will render a detector as deaf as no bias at all. Note also that it is possible to bias a detector in the wrong direction. If advancing the potentiometer does not result in increased sensitivity, the battery terminals should be swapped, so as to reverse the polarity of the bias volt

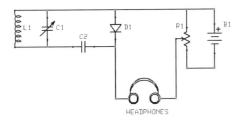

Figure 4

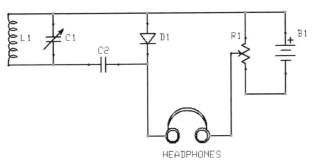

HEADPHONES

Figure 5

age. The circuit shown in Figure 5 is interesting in this context, because it is capable of applying either a positive or negative bias, of varying magnitude, without rewiring the battery.

Where can one find samples of minerals to experiment with? I checked the phone directory listings for a half-dozen major cities in the United States, and each revealed several rock and mineral shops where detector materials might be purchased. If brick-and-mortar shops are not your cup of tea, minerals are offered for sale through numerous Internet retailers including giants like Amazon and Ebay.

A Google search of the phrase "minerals for sale" yields more than ten million hits. In this day and age, the Internet may be the best place to begin any search of this type.

I am fortunate to live in Tucson, Arizona, host of the annual International Gem and Mineral Show. Each year, hundreds of vendors converge on our city to offer for sale a staggering variety of mineral specimens, collected from the four corners of the earth. This event takes place between mid-January and mid-February of each year. If you happen to be the inhabitant of a state or province that is normally snow-bound at that time of year, the search for radio detector minerals can provide a wonderful excuse to visit and enjoy Tucson's warmth and hospitality.

If all else fails, poke around in the dirt in your backyard, at the park, a hiking trail, or on the beach. You might be surprised what you find.

Below is a list of some of the information sources cited in this article. I also invite you to visit my website at: www.hpfriedrichs.com

Bucher, Elmer. Practical Wireless Telegraphy. New York: Wireless Press, 1921.

Corrigan, J.F. Crystal Experimenter's Handbook. ??: Popular Wireless, 1925.

Coursey, Philip. Telephony Without Wires. London: The Wireless Press Ltd, 1919.

Friedrichs, H.P. Instruments of Amplification. Tucson, AZ: H.P. Friedrichs, 2003.

Friedrichs, H.P. The Voice of the Crystal. Tucson, AZ: H.P. Friedrichs, 1999.

Gabel, Victor. "The Crystal as a Generator and Amplifier." Wireless World & Radio Review. October 1, 1924:p2

Garten, Justin. "Splatter." QST Magazine. October, 1944:p86

Kujanpaa, Toivo. "Strays." QST Magazine. July, 1944:p62

Lange, Norbert Adoph. Handbook of Chemistry. Sandusky, OH: Handbook Publishers, 1956.

Morgan, Alfred. Wireless Telegraph Construction For Amateurs. New York: D. Van Nostrand Co., 1913.

Pellant, Chris. Rocks and Minerals. New York: DK Publishing, 1992.

Stranger, Ralph. Wireless The Modern Magic Carpet. London: Partridge Press, 1928.

Toricata, Wichi. "Commerical Wireless Telegraphy in Japan." Electrician. September 16, 1910:p??

Useful Primitive Radio Detector Minerals

Mineral	Chemical Composition	Chemical Formula	Crystal Category	Suitable Contacts	PW (1925)	Eccles (1928)	Toricata (1910)	Morgan (1913)
Allemontite	Arsenic antimonide	AsSb	Antimonide				x	
Anatase	Titanium dioxide	TiO2	Oxide	Metals and Zincite	x		x	
Antimony	Element	Sb	Element	Zincite, silicon, etc.	x			
Argentite (silver glance)	Silver sulfide	Ag2S	Sulfide	Metals, graphite, tellurium	x			
Arkansite	See Anatase							
Arsenic	Element	As	Element	Metals and Zincite	x	x	x	
Arsenic pyrites	See Mispickel						x	
Bornite (peacock ore)	Sulfide of copper and iron	Cu5FeS4	Sulfide	Zincite, silicon, etc.	x	x	x	x
Boron	Element	B	Element	Zincite, tellurium	x	x		
Boulangerite	Sulfide of antimony and lead	Pb5Sb4S11	Sulfosalt	Zincite, tellurium, antimony, bismuth	x		x	
Bourmonite	Sulfide of copper, antimony and lead	PbCuSbS3	Sulfosalt		x			
Brookite	See Anatase					x		x
Carborundum	Silicon Carbide	SiC	Sulfide	Steel, zincite	x			
Chalcopyrite	Sulfide of iron and copper	CuFeS2	Sulfide	Zincite (this combination is the famous Perikon detector)	x	x		x
Cobaltite	Cobalt arsenic sulfide	CoAsS	Sulfide	Zincite	x		x	
Cassiterite	Tin Oxide	SnO2	Oxide	Metals	x		x	
Cerussite	Lead Carbonate	PbCo3	Carbonate	?		x		
Chalcocite (copper glance)	Copper sulfide	Cu2S	Sulfide	Zincite, tellurium	x	x	x	
Copper pyrites	Sulfide of iron and copper	CuFeS2	Sulfide	Zincite (this combination is the famous Perikon detector)	x		x	
Corundum	Aluminum oxidde	Al2O3	Oxide	Zincite, bornite	x			
Covellite	Copper sulfide	CuS	Sulfide	Zincite, etc	x		x	

Mineral	Description	Formula	Class	Tellurium, antimony, etc	X1	X2	X3	X4	X5
(Cuprous oxide)	Copper oxide	Cu2O	Oxide				x	x	
Domeykite	Copper arsenide	Cu3As	Arsenide		x	x			x
Enargite	Sulfide of copper and arsenic	Cu3AsS4	Sulfosalt			x			
Erubescite	See Bornite						x		
Frieslebenite	Sulfide of antimony, silver, and lead	PbAgSbS3 (composition varies)	Sulfide	Zincite, silicon		x	x		x
Galena	Lead sulfide	PbS	Sulfide	Metals, graphite, galena, silicon	x	x	x	x	
Graphite	Element	C	Element	Zincite, galena, molybendite, silicon		x	x	x	
Hematite	Iron Oxide	Fe2O3	Oxide	Zincite, most sulfide materials			x		
Hessite	Telluride of silver or gold					x			x
Hystatite	See Ilmenite					x	x		
Ilmenite	Oxide of iron and titanium	FeTiO3	Oxide	Metals, silicon		x	x		
Iridosmine	Native alloy of iridium and osmium	Composition varies	Alloy			x			
Iserine	See Ilmenite					x			
Iron Pyrites	Iron sulfide	FeS2	Sulfide	Metals, silicon, zincite, tellurium	x	x	x	x	x
Lollingite	Iron arsenide	FeAs2 plus other metals	Arsenide			x	x		
Magnetite	Magnetic iron oxide	Fe3O4	Oxide	Silicon, carbon, etc		x	x		
Marcasite	Iron sulfide (containing arsenic)	FeS2 with As	Sulfide	Similar to iron pyrites	x	x	x		
Melaconite	See Tenorite					x			
Meteorite	Iron/Nickel mixture	Composition varies	Alloy			x	x		
Mispickel	Sulfide of iron and arsenic	FeAsS2	Sulfide	Similar to iron pyrites			x		

Mineral	Chemical Composition	Chemical Formula	Crystal Category	Suitable Contacts	PW (1925)	Eccles (1928)	Toricata (1910)	Morgan (1913)
Molybdenite	Molybdenum sulfide	MoS2	Sulfide	Silver, graphite	x	x	x	x
Nagyagite		Pb5A(Te,Sb)4 S5-8	Sulfosalt				x	
Niccolite	Nickel arsenide	NiAs	Arsenide				x	
Octahedrite	See Anatase							x
Plattnerite	Lead peroxide	PbO2	Oxide	Lead	x			x
Psilomelane	Manganese oxide	Mn2O3H2O	Oxide	Zincite, metals	x	x	x	
Pyrolusite	Manganese dioxide	MnO2	Oxide	Zincite, metals	x		x	
Pyrrhotite	See Iron Pyrites				x		x	
Schwatzitge	Compound of copper, lead, antimony and arsenic	Composition varies					x	
Siegenite	Nickel cobalt sulfide	(Ni,Co)3S4	Sulfide				x	
Silicon	Element	Si	Element	Metals, zincite, iron pyrites, etc	x	x		x
Smaltine (Smaltite)	Arsenide of cobalt, iron and nickel	(Co,Fe,Ni)As2	Arsenide	?		x	x	
Stannite	Mixture of iron, copper, and tin sulfides	Composition varies						
Stibnite	Antimony sulfide	Sb2S3	Sulfide	Zincite, etc	x			
Stromeyerite	Sulfide of copper and silver	CuAgS	Sulfide	Zincite, etc	x			x
Strutterudite	Cobalt arsenide with nickel and iron	(Co,Ni,Fe)As3	Arsenide	Zincite and some metals			x	
Sylvanite	Silver gold telluride	(Ag,Au)Te2	Telluride				x	
Tantalum	Element	Ta	Element	Mercury				x
Tellurium	Element	Te	Element	Zincite, aluminum, silicon	x	x		
Tennantie	Sulfide of copper iron and arsenic	(Cu,Fe)12As4 S13	Sulfosalt				x	
Tenorite (Copper Oxide)	Copper oxide	CuO	Oxide				x	
Tin pyrites	See Stannite							
Ullmanite	Nickel arsenic sulfide	NiAsS	Sulfide				x	
Wad	Manganese oxides or hydroxides	Composition varies	Oxide or hydroxide				x	
Zinc blende (sphalerite)	Sulfide of zinc and iron	(Zn,Fe)S	Sulfide		x	x	x	
Zincite	Zinc oxide, containing manganese	ZnO	Oxide	Almost any contact	x	x	x	x

Now Hear This!
by Dan Petersen, W7OIL

Elmer Oldham was engaged in one of his favorite activities, napping in front of his favorite HRO senior receiver, "cans" on his head and his hand ready next to the "bug" he liked to use. In his reverie he hears "NOW HEAR THIS! GENERAL QUARTERS! ENEMY SPOTTED!!" He awoke with a start and went for the bug when he realized that he had been dreaming. "Well", he thought, "So much for the Big War." Then he saw The Young Ham's head sticking up through the trapdoor in the floor of the attic and he invited Robin up. "You're sweating, Mr. Oldham" was Robin's first observation. "Just a sec." Elmer replied, "I need to take these cans off - they start hurtin' after a while!"

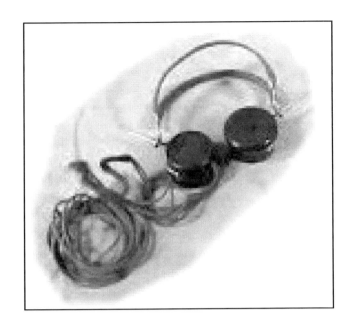

"Cans?" the Young Ham asked. "Yeah", Elmer said. "Baldy's - Headphones" - "You know you are a real radio operator when you can pull off a full watch with these on without getting a headache. My childhood nickname was "Jughead" because my ears stuck 'way out - until my stint in the Navy. Spending the War with cans flattening my ears took care of that nickname." He scratched one ear that was now permanently flattened against his head.

Headphones, along with the almost obsolete slang term "cans" have been a staple from their invention early in the 20th century to today's "MP3" players. They take many forms but they all serve the same purpose - to conduct sound directly to the user's ears efficiently. They also provide a degree of privacy for the wearer but the real advantage is that they do not require much energy to work. This is where their use with crystal and regenerative radios comes to the fore.

The idea of the "telephone transducer" was popularized by the experiments and inventions of folks like Edison, Elisha Grey and A. G. Bell. In 1910 Nathaniel Baldwin in Utah developed two of these transducers incorporated with a headband and sent a prototype to Lt. Comdr. A. J. Hepburn of the U.S. Navy. Hepburn found them very useful and ordered more. Baldwin could only furnish ten at a time as he was building them in his kitchen! Nathaniel Baldwin's phones went on to become one of the most premier headphones of the mid-century and whose 'phones are highly prized to this day.

So, Where to begin? First of all, how do they operate? A headphone converts electrical energy into mechanical motion which in turn generates sound energy. The earliest and most common form was the "dynamic" headphone or "telephone" as it was known early on. The electrical energy was passed through a coil wound around a magnet. This creates a "biased" electromagnet which attracts magnetic materials such as an iron diaphragm. The diaphragm is very thin and will deform depending on the amount of current passing through the coil. If the current varies at an audio

rate the diaphragm will follow the changes in current and create sound waves. The coil can also be connected directly to the diaphragm with the coil "floating" in a magnetic field. Figure 1 is a representation of how they are made.

Another version is the "piezoelectric" or "crystal" headphone. Figure 2 shows how the "innards" are arranged. This type utilizes the property of a specially ground crystal. The piezoelectric effect is that when a voltage is impressed on two certain points on the crystal the crystal will deform more or less depending on the voltage applied. The crystal is mechanically linked to a diaphragm. The vibrations thus induced create sound waves. These phones can be very sensitive but are also delicate. Dropping them on the floor is not recommended but they are quite rugged enough for normal use.

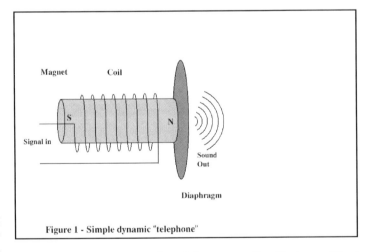

Figure 1 - Simple dynamic "telephone"

A third type, and considered by many the "holy grail" of headphones is the "balanced armature" headphone. Figure 3 reveals that this style is more complex than the other two but it pays off in increased sensitivity than the other "dynamic" style. Note that the coil is wound around a core

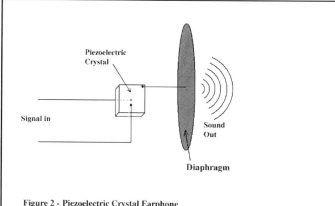

Figure 2 - Piezoelectric Crystal Earphone

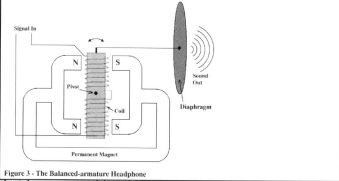

Figure 3 - The Balanced-armature Headphone

that is supported by a pivot and suspended in a magnetic field. Baldwin headphones and "sound-powered" phones use this concept to achieve their superior sensitivity. They are however more scarce than the Figure 1 dynamic style and more expensive when you DO find them.

My reader may have heard of "sound-powered" phones. When I was a kid there were barrels of them at the war-surplus store for just a couple of bucks each. They were heavy and uncomfortable not to mention looking "dorky" so they stayed in their barrels. The same type of "element" is used both for listening and talking. Talking into the element generates a voltage that the "receive" element converts back to sound. Batteries not included as batteries are not needed. No power source other than your voice. These are still used on board ships since as long as there is wire continuity between the elements they will work. These phones are prized now for their exquisite sensitvity but you need a fat wallet to get a pair.

A Word or Two About Impedance:

The term "impedance" is bandied about a lot. High-impedance is the word we are looking for. Many 'phones are rated at about 2000 ohms. This is not the DC resistance but a combination of that and the reactance at a particular audio frequency. Hence it can be a little vague. The "ear-buds" used in modern music players are low to medium impedance meaning usually less than 600 ohms. Not good for crystal radios. Crystal earphones are essentially infinite impedance. Electrically they "look" like a capacitor so a parallel resistor is used to act as a resistive load. Witout this resistor, usually 10,000 to 68,000 ohms value, the audio will

be weak and distorted. As dynamic and balanced-armature headphones DO have a DC resistance they do not require a load resistor.

Representative Types:

The most simple type of dynamic head-phone can run the gamut of "darn good" to "deaf as Beethoven". I have found that the "Trimm Dependable" dynamic head-phones are dependably

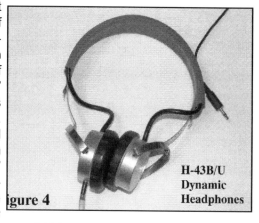

H-43B/U Dynamic Headphones

Figure 4

mediocre. They are OK but nothing to write home about. "Telex" phones are usually low impedance but I did at one time have a 2000 ohm pair. I wasn't impressed. Much better are the H-43B/U headphones I picked up from eBay a few years ago. These were touted as "Korean Army Headphones". They are actually 3000 ohm units made for use with a Radiac Geiger Counter. They are quite sensitive but they come with a caveat - do NOT attempt to take them apart. A friend of mine did and ruined the unit. I paid $30.00 several years ago for a "new in the bag" set.

Next on the list is the Nathaniel Baldwin "Type-C" balanced armature headphone. A clue that they are balanced armature is the deep "cans" containing the elements. The interior magnet takes up more room than a simple dynamic pair like Figure 4. For headphones

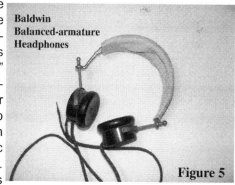

Baldwin Balanced-armature Headphones

Figure 5

that are not in the "sound-powered" category they are excellent. The pair I own were in pretty poor shape when I got them. I made a new deerskin headband and polished off the bird-droppings and cleaned dead spiders out of the "cans". A new cotton-covered cord and they are good to go! If you see Baldwin phones at a fleamarket they would be well worth picking up.

The sound-powered headphone - The one representative I have is a pair of British "DLR-5" headphones. Reputedly made by Mullard (and probably others) they are WW2 vintage. The "DLR" is rumored to mean "Dynamic Low Resistance" and they do have a low DC resistance. My pair reads 56 ohms but that does not mean they are low *impedance.* I find they are best used with a hammond organ impedance matching transformer where you can juggle taps to get the best impedance match to your set. They are VERY sensitive. In Figure 6 I am holding them by their fabric headband. The stiff wire around the back is to hold the cans apart while you put them on. It seems strange but they are quite comfortable when you get them arranged on your

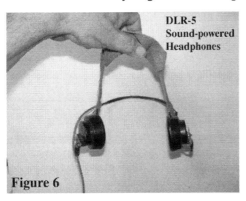

DLR-5 Sound-powered Headphones

Figure 6

head. These can be found on the internet but bring a wallet full of money.

And Now, Closer to Home...

There are a couple of sets I keep here that are pretty easy on your wallet and well worth the money. The first is from our own Xtal Set Society in the form of the Crystal Earphone, illustrated in Figure 7. Note I call them "ear" phones and not "head" phones. These are inserted into your ear-canal rather than pressed to your head with a headband. They were originally developed in the 1950's for hearing aids. The best ones are the old Japanese made ones but the current ones are practically as good. When I use them I use two. I find they cut out outside noise and kind of balance the sound in the middle of my head. Remember to use them with a load resistor or you will find the audio weak and fuzzy. This is caused by the fact that electrically they are a capacitor and will charge up. It sounds like someone talking with a mouth full of mashed potatoes, which may not be a bad analogy. In the sensitivity department they are pretty dog-gone good. These little beauties are available from The XSS catalog on-line .

Last on the list but certainly not least is the "Peebles Originals" piezoelectric headphones. Figure 8 shows and if they look like a pair of hearing-protectors you are right. Through the genius of Peebles engineering he takes this meek pair of hearing protectors and inserts high-quality piezoelectric elements. The result is a great pair of earphones that nears the sensitivity of the rare sound-powered phones. They are also *very* comfortable and block out external noise like - well, a pair of hearing protectors! They are available through the "Peebles Original's" website.

If you are trolling for headphones at a fleamarket it would be handy to take an ohm-meter with you. You can check the DC resistance of them and see if you hear a "click" in the elements. Choosing the right headphone is a personal thing. I know one person will say that such-and-such a pair ain't worth the effort to throw them out while someone else will say that same make is the best they ever used. Get what works best for you.

Happy experimenting!

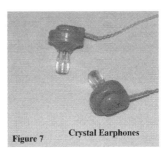

Figure 7   Crystal Earphones

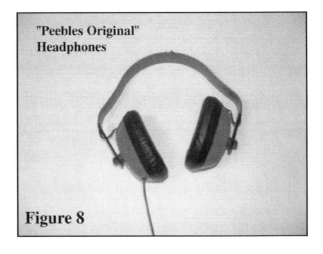

"Peebles Original" Headphones

Figure 8

Editor note:
The pictures here are from Larry Jeffers. It seems that Dan is not the only one thinking of earphones. Larry says the single phone works well, but the double in series is great!

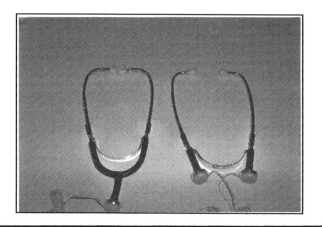
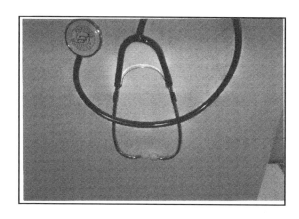

The Multi Loop Antenna

For those of you who do not know me I am Chuck Young, KA8WOT. I have a Beagle named Lady and a male cat named Red. Every day I ask Lady if we should have this for supper today. If Lady does not say anything, after three tries, I pick something else for supper until Lady barks, "Yes." at that choice. Almost always when I am asking Lady what we should have for supper Red cries, "Tuna fish." Usually Lady does not agree with Red but every now and then Lady will agree with Red and we have tuna fish for supper that day. For medical reasons I have to eat and take medications and eat at: 8:00AM, noon, 4:00PM and 8:00PM.

Lady and I were on our way home from Skidway Lake, where we had helped Dale, AB8BU, SK, with another Mills Township Fourth Of July Parade. Lady and I were bouncing around ideas on how to make a fullwave loop antenna better. As we were going down Pinnacle Hill towards Pinnacle Bridge over the Rifle River Lady asked, "What about the feeding of the fan dipole?" That was it! Lady had hit the nail on the head. We set out to test the theory.

In the fan dipole you have a: 160m dipole, 80m dipole, 40m dipole, 20m dipole, 15m dipole and 10m dipole all fed at a common center insulator. If you feed a fan dipole with good 50 ohm coax, it will work very well. If you feed a fan dipole with 75 ohm coax, running fifteen- hundred watts into it will not work as well as one-hundred watts into a dipole fed with good 50 ohm coax.

As an experiment we put up some posts made of two eight foot two by fours in the ground two feet leaving the top of the post six feet up. I had a fullwave loop and dipole for 160m up and I moved the fullwave loop over to. the top of the posts. Now I knew the fullwave loop would receive better by two S-units better than the halfwave dipole did. With the tops of the 160m fullwave loop only six foot off the ground that fullwave loop was receiving two S-units weaker than the halfwave dipole. It appeared that the fullwave loop just had to be further off the ground so we went to eight feet. Not high enough. At ten feet high the fullwave loop started working like it should. We chose to run the posts tops up to thirteen feet six inches off the ground since that was with only six inches of overlap on each eight foot sections. Changing the feed point of the Multi Loop Antenna did not have any effect on the radiation pattern. A rectangle acted like a rectangle and a square acted like a square.

All the lower sections of supports are made the same way with two eight foot two by fours. Opinions as to what to use what to stop bugs abound. My personal view starts with a good oil based enamel paint. Although we were only going to put two foot of the post in the ground I decided-to-paint the bottom three feet of the post-The first two coats of paint I put on before the bottom two eight foot two by fours were put together. The most economic way to join these two by fours is with four sixteen penny nails.

Put the two by fours together to form a T. About a half of foot, six inches, fifteen centimeters, from the bottom and from the top put a nail in to hold the top of the T to the vertical part of the T. About two foot, twenty-four inches, sixty-one centimeters, from each nail you drive your other two nails. Once you have made the T you need to paint the bottom three feet of post with three more coats of your good oil based enamel paint. Five coats of a good oil based enamel paint will put a really bad taste in most bugs that live below ground so they will protect very well. For protection on something with enamel paint you want the coats to be as thick as you can make them but they need to be fully dry before the next coat on top of it. The spots where the nail heads are you should make sure there are a full five coats on them too.

The top sections are done almost the same way. The closes the top section is to the ground is five and a half feet. One of the places you want a nail is in the center of the eight foot long section. The top sections for the 160m and 40m fullwave loops are made the same way. The reason the 40m top sections are made as strong and the 160m fullwave loop is because the 40m top sections hold up the: 40m, 20m, 15m and 10m fullwave loops inside them. You need eight of the top sections unless you want to do something other than a square or rectangle for your Multi Loop Antenna. For several years I ran a fullwave loop in a triangle with my major nulls to the north and south. Every time I checked in to this Net there was this Ham the lived due south of me and he could never hear me even with fifteen-hundred watts or power. Then one day Lady and I decided that we should make that fullwave loop into a square so we did. I had the power turned down to five watts on my Kenwood TS-2000X for testing. That Ham to the south of me was taking the checkins for the Net and I was sure he was not going to be able to hear me so I keyed the microphone and tossed out my call letters. Right off the bat, first try, that Ham to the south on me heard me. From that time on, unless there was a thunderstorm someplace, I only ran five watts on that Net. Later on several Hams said, "You have the weakest signal on the band but you are loudest person on the band." Because of the noise in here, when the air conditioner is on, I get real close to the microphone and talk a little louder.

You will need to cut nine inches, three/quarters of a foot, twenty-two point eight-six centimeters, off of each of the eight two by fours. On the other eight two by fours you mark each one of them six inches, one half foot, fifteen point two four centimeters, up from one end. Take one of the two by fours with the nine inches cut off it and make the vertical piece of the T section. Line up the end of the shorter two by four so one end of it is at the six inch mark on the horizontal part of the T second and nail it in place. G~ to the other end of the T section and the vertical part will be three inches from the top, nail it in place. You should use at least five sixteen penny nails to hold the top T section together. If you want to use lag bolts in place of sixteen penny nails, they will work well here but use a flat washer under their heads.

Joining the top section to the bottom section you might need a little help holding them in place to get them started. For each post you will need: two one/quarter inch bolts long enough to go through both thickness' on your two by fours plus a half inch, two nuts for these bolts, four flat washers and two lock washers. You will need a quarter inch drill long enough to go through both thickness' of the your two by fours. On the bottom of the top section, the end with six inches of overhang, mark one inch up from the bottom and one/half inch in from each side, this is where you will drill your holes for the bolts.

You will need a couple of the nine inch blocks that you cut off to make the shorter pieces. If you happen to have a bench sixteen feet long, use it. If not, a garage floor will work just fine. You can use a relatively flat piece of ground for this part.

Place a bottom section on the ground. At the top of the bottom section place the bottom end, the place where there is six inches before the T section starts, so that the six inches overlaps the bottom section: Place the two nine inch long blocks so each one of them is flat, one about a foot up from where the two sections meet and the other about a foot from the top of the top section.

Get the drill ready. While balancing the bottom T section place the top T section so it is on top of the bottom section. While pushing the two balanced T sections together drill the holes in the places that you have marked. Just as soon as the hole is drilled put in one of the quarter inch bolts and a flat washer. Then drill the other hole and put the bolt and flat washer in it. One guy decided that he was going to use a six foot level to make sure the sections were straight but it took three more people to deal with the six foot level. Take a sixteen penny nail and put it in the middle of the top section five inches up from the bottom of the top section and drive it home there. If you wish the use a lag bolt in place of a sixteen penny nail, that will work just ~e. ~ut a: flat washer, a lock washer and a nut on each of the bolts. Only tighten the nuts until the flat washers are even with the wood. Any tighter is not good for the wood.

On the top three inches of the overhang you need the cut slot for your sting or rope that you are going to use. I use number eighteen nylon string. It will hold up the 160m fullwave loop and when the wind is blowing so hard that it blows out a propane torch, it is twenty degree below zero with a wind chill factor that will make you think you are at The South Pole I find it a lot easier to tie the string back together again than it is to solder the antenna back together. Oh yeah, he string breaks before the eighteen gauge copperweld antenna wire that I use. I have a crosscut saw that leaves just a wide enough path that the string I use just fits into it nicely. If you wish to use quarter inch rope for you 40m, 20m, 15m and 10m fullwave loops you should probably use a piece of two by four at least four inches long on the top of the 40m, 20m, 15, and 10m fullwave loops sections.

Now that you have one post for the 160m fullwave loop or the: 40m, 20m, 15m and 10m fullwave loops you have to decide what you are going to do with it. My fist posts I did nothing but paint the bottom three feet to keep the bugs away. You need to address the problems of rain, snow, sleet and other weather related things like sunshine in the summertime. If all you are going to do is seal it, use the best sealer you can buy in liquid form, not the spray can. With a two inch paintbrush put a good heavy coat of sealer on it in the morning. Wait until the next morning to put the second coat of sealer on it. Wait until the next morning to put the third coat of sealer on it. Wait until the next morning to put the fourth coat of sealer on it. Wait until the next day to use them. If you follow these instructions, you will be glad you did.

I worked for this place that was going to add a machine shop to their building and when it came to sealing the concrete the guy in charge of taking care of everything told them but buy the best sealer that money could buy. They took his advice and everyone was happy that the sealer they used. Several years later they needed to add on to the machine shop but they opted for the cheapest concrete sealer they could find. It made such a mess that they had to come in and take up four inches of the concrete and put down fresh cement. That time they spent the money for the best sealer money could buy and neve~ questioned the guy in charge of keep the place up again. That same goes for the wood sealers on the market. I know this guy who was talked into putting down this stuff on his deck that had a thirty year warranty to it, I told him to get the good stuff and he told be that was the best wood sealer in the world. Three years later he was ripping up his deck and had to put new wood down. I asked, "How did that sealer work for you." He was so mad that he could not talk. I tell the truth and people hate me for it. Same thing is with paint. The ninety-nine cent can of spray paint is not going to protect what you are going to want to protect it from. You have to choose: looks good or protects good. Protection for wood outside is with a paintbrush in the form of a good oil based enamel paint. The same paint you used on the bottom three feet of the post. A different color, if you like, but the protection will be there if you get a good five coats on it. I built my first 80m dipole antenna in 1964 so I have seen how things hold up. At one time, I was told, you had the replace your antenna at least every five years. It was not until I let an antenna go for ten years and when I went to use it again I did not have to do anything to it but check the SWR which was just fine.

Like with any antenna the higher you get it off the ground the better it will work. This is to get it off the ground high enough for it to work well enough to make your efforts worthwhile. One Ham decided that we was going to use four sixty foot towers he had to string up a Multi Loop Antenna with and he was so surprised that he did not believe his S-meter when compared to his dipole antenna on 80m. If you like a fullwave loop that has been put up and fed properly, you will love the Multi Loop Antenna. On the average day take the Ham who was pushing your S-meter to an S-five on your fullwave loop, he will be an S-seven on the Multi Loop Antenna. The S-zero noise on your fullwave loop will be even quieter on the Multi Loop Antenna.

The last time I was on 160m and there were static crashes that were pushing my S-meter to S-five on the Multi

Loop Antenna everybody on that frequency was getting of the static crashes, one Ham with a halfwave dipole said he was getting 30dB over S-nine static crashes. The weakest signal I was getting on them was an S-six so I could hear him very well. I do not have a 160m antenna up other than the Multi Loop Antenna so I could not switch antennas to see how it was working. I barrowed an 80m fullwave loop to put up so I could report on how the Multi Loop Antenna was working next to that. Then some Hams wanted me to put up a halfwave dipole for 80m just so I could report on that.

With the Multi Loop Antenna in a square the major nulls are: northeast, southeast, southwest and northwest. The major nulls are 4.2SdB deeper than the major nulls on the fullwave loop by itself In my opinion, I think: Kenwood put the worst automatic tuner they ever made in my TS-2000X. However my TS-2000X can tune the Multi Loop Antenna from 160m through 6m. I did not intend on using the Multi Loop Antenna on 6m but here is how it happened.

The TS-2000X has two HF through 6m antenna ports. There is a receive only HF antenna port that I have only used just to make sure that part of the radio was working right when I first got my TS-2000X which happened to be a gift from my mother. I was testing the automatic antenna tuner in the TS-2000X to see what it would tune on 6m with only five watts of power into the Multi Loop Antenna and there was a band opening on 6m. I heard this Ham calling CQ so, without thinking, I keyed the microphone and tossed my call letters at him. He could hear me. He gives me his QTH and I reach for the rotor control box so I can turn my homebrewed four element vertical yagi at him. As the rotor is turning my S-meter is not picking up any better like it should be because I was getting closer to being pointed at him with the beam. Then I remembered that I was only running five watts on the Multi Loop Antenna. Well he was horizontally polarized and when I did get the vertical yagi pointed at him he was stronger on the Multi Loop Antenna. I worked several Hams on that band opening and if they were horizontal I picked them up better and they picked me up better on the Multi Loop Antenna. Vertical was a different story, the four element vertical yagi worked better than the Multi Loop Antenna.

I have never been a fan of the GSRV antenna for the simple fact that using a halfwave dipole for each band would always out perform the GSRV antenna. Since I

have been using the Multi Loop Antenna is feels good to have an antenna that will cover from 160m through 6m is something that I have gotten use to. The major nulls are something that I can live with and that is the only down side of the project.

Feeding the Multi Loop Antenna is as easy as you want to make it. A good low loose fifty ohm coax is good and the automatic antenna tuner in the TS-2000X will handle that. I am using :fifty feet of RG/8X If you wish to use 450 ohm twinlead, you will need a better antenna tuner than the TS-2000X has in it. If you use 450 ohm twinlead, you should put a PL-259 on the end of it and do not use a balun.

The Multi Loop Antenna is the best HF/6m horizontal almost omnidirectional antenna I have ever used and I have built every antenna that someone has come up with.

From the Johnson Smith & Co Catalog. Looks a bit like the Philmore detector we found.

Revisiting the Henry-O-Meter
By Phil, WØXI

James Hawes, AA9DT, sent us a note a while back about the "Henry-O-Meter" article that appeared in 73 Magazine forty plus years ago written by WA8MLP. We have to agree with James about the wealth of information packed into those old 73 back issues; Wayne's magazine is no longer published and that's too bad. I simulated the CB (common base) PNP oscillator circuit described using LTspice (a software program) and could not get it to work either. I suspect there are wiring errors in the original schematic and some component values were missing. Still, the idea is interesting. I've redrawn the schematic in the article without change as Figure 1.

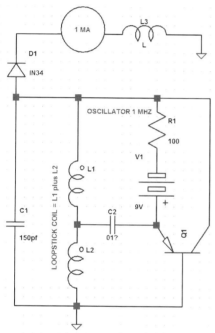

Figure 1

Here's the author's idea behind the meter. "The Henryometer is based on the formula for inductive reactance. This states that the two variables which control reactance are frequency and inductance. Since the meter supplies the frequency, inductance will control reactance. Thus the circuit is a reactance or AC ohmmeter." Saying this another way, if we apply an RF voltage (a steady sine wave) of a given frequency across a pure coil, the resulting sinusoidal current will be dependent upon the voltage and coil inductance. Given that the voltage applied is constant (in peak to peak value and frequency), the current obtained will go down as the value of the inductance is increased

and vice versa. This relationship of L (inductance) and I (the current) could then be used to label the panel of the milliamp meter with inductance values.

Here is the author's test procedure. "To test a coil, connect it across the terminals. Momentarily short the leads and adjust the control (we assume he means the pot) for zero, or one mA, undo the short and read the value (in uH) indicated." The picture of his homebrew unit showed his MA meter face marked up for uH values from 0.25 to 10 mH.

Assuming the original frequency of operation was 1 MHz and C1 was 150 pf, the total inductance of the loop stick (coil) when seem to have been ~ 170 uH, or 85 uH per section for L1 and L2. The text indicated that there was a pot somewhere in the circuit; and, I assume that it applies to the only resistor in the circuit, R1. James thinks it might have been a pot placed in series with the 1 MA meter (but left out of the schematic). The author used a DC MA meter to measure the current and in order to do that he put a 1N34 diode (D1) between the oscillator voltage source and the meter and coil under test.

Before filing these notes, I decided to simulate NPN and PNP versions of the Common Collector Hartley Oscillator, using LT-Spice, and did get them to work. Theses schematics are shown in Figures 2 and 3.

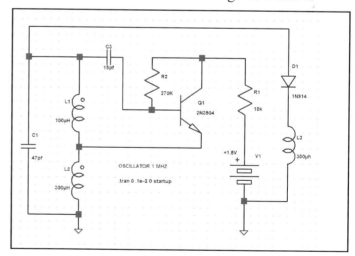

Figure 2

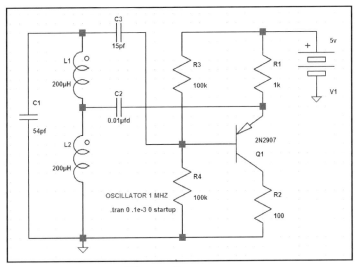

Figure 3

Let's take a closer look at the PNP oscillator, Figure 3. The feedback for oscillation is controlled by the ratio of L1 to L2. The smaller L1 is compared to L2 the less the feedback and the smaller the output voltage (at the top of L1). The frequency is set by L1, L2, C1 and a small amount of capacitance from coupling cap C3. A slight tweak in C1 gave me the 1 MHz of oscillation I was after. The simulation is also interesting in that the trace in figure 4 shows how the oscillator comes up to speed after battery power is supplied.

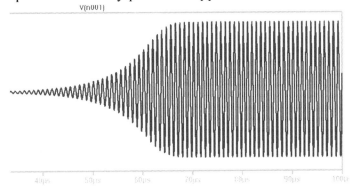

Figure 4

I then attached a diode and inductor in series (like that of Figure 1) to see what the current through a test inductor would look like. As I suspected, the waveform was distorted. I think the original circuit for measuring the current in the inductor via a DC meter needs to be changed if possible.

Given that, I decided to measure the current using a signal generator, sensing resistor, and oscilloscope. Most coils used in AM band circuits are small and fall

into the 30 to 300 micro-henry (uH) range, I decided to measure a 220 uH and a 150 uH, which are standard values and in my stock.

My measurement circuit consisted of a coil in series with a 10 ohm ¼-watt sensing resistor, as noted in Figure 5. The leads coming from the generator connect to the left side of the coil and to the ground strip at the bottom. I then added the 10 ohm resistor in series with the coil. The far right side of the resistor is then connected to ground. The jig is a simple series circuit starting with the signal generator, set at 8 volts peak to peak (VPP) at a frequency of 1 MHz. The generator scope trace is shown in Figure 6. The oscilloscope was then used to confirm the voltage at the node between the coil and resistor, i.e. across the sensing resistor and ground. The voltage was 60 mv so the current was 60/10 or 6 ma. The two voltages and frequency were then used to calculate the inductance of the coil under test.

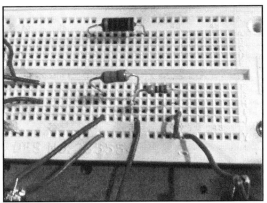

Figure 5

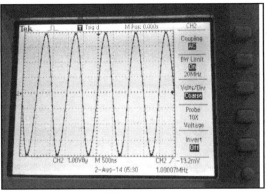

Figure 6

The theory behind this scheme is as follows. First, think of how you use a voltmeter to measure the voltage between two resistors connected in series. The cur rent is the same in both resistors. So, you can measure the voltage across either resistor and then calculate the current following through both.

When it comes to AC circuits, those including a capacitor and/or inductor with a resistor, things get a bit messy. Our circuit wired above includes just one 220uH coil and one 10 ohm resistor. Second, the AC impedance of a coil, called its reactance, is equal to $2\pi f$ times its inductance, also written as XL, where X is equal to $2\pi f$, f being the frequency of operation. And here's the trick: we'll make our sensing resistor very small so that it barely affects the resulting current in the circuit. Then we can estimate the inductance (AC impedance) of the coil by first measuring the AC current through the 10 ohm sensing resistor. For our 220 uH coil, its impedance (reactance) is calculated as follows:

AC Ohms Law goes as follows: $V=X*I$, where X is $2\pi f*L$, so $V=2\pi f * L * I$, rearranging :

$$L = \frac{V}{2\pi f I} = \frac{8vpp}{2\pi * 1Mhz * 60 / 10ma} = 212uH.$$

Using ohms law and a voltmeter or scope we measure the voltage across our sensing resistor and calculate the current (which is also the current through the coil). Using the current in the circuit, the frequency of the current (and voltage applied) and the voltage across the coil (disregarding the small voltage drop across the sensing resistor), we can calculate the inductance.

Notice that this result is very close to the value printed on the part. I ran a second measurement for the 150 uH coils and got 149.8. Nice!

If you found this stuff interesting and want to look at the original 73 article, search for henryometer on the web.

Xtal Corner: Member Correspondence 2014

From Carl Fleming:
 Would you know if I could use a 2N43a transistor in a home made transistor radio or should I use a 2N107 type? I have read that the PNP 2N107 was very popular in the early days of transistor radios.

Hello Carl,
The 2N43a and 2N107 were introduced in 1953 and 1955 respectively by General Electric. $2 was considered cheap at the time for the "inched top" or "tophat" style 2N107 and it was taughted as designed for hobby use, since they were seconds off the production line of the 2N4x series. That says to me that one would want to go with the 2N4x series. These transistors are germanium based point contact and PNP as you mentioned.

It might be interested to tie the base and collector together and thus try the 2N4x as a diode in a crystal set, making the base-collector one lead and the emitter the other! For more history on this, see this internet web address:
http://semiconductormuseum.com/PhotoGallery/PhotoGallery_2N107.htm

I just keyed in a search for "PNP germanium transistors" on the Mouser.com website and came up with one To-92 package, Mouser's part no. 512MPSH81. There are several thousand left on this "end of life" part.
Phil

Dear Rebecca and the team,
 Having read the November Newsletter , I just had to write and congratulate Dan Petersen for such a lucid explanation of Valves/tubes During my period as a radio apprentice (I worked in a small shop when radios were still repairable) In the 1960's I was sent to "College" one day a week to learn, or be taught radio theory. Transistors had arrived by that time, in UK? No ! Still teaching tube/valve theory and I just didn't get it at the age of 15. The teacher was obviously bored ,and so was I. His English accent called them volves.

Dan has come along and explained, and after fifty years the theory has finally sunk in. Congratulations to you all . Fifty years! And it took Dan 20 minutes to put me right.
All best wishes, Nick Collis Bird. Dorset . UK.

From James

Hi, I have a need for an air variable cap like the one you sell. But, I need for Counterclockwise to be low capacitance, and clockwise high capacitance.

I am thinking that I can remove the "stop bar" on the blades to allow them to rotate 360 degrees. I can then line up the pointer on my knob to be low cap on zero, and high cap on 100. I will just have to put stops on the ends of the vernier that the pointer will hit to keep it from going too far. Does this make sense ?   Or as an alternative, do you know of somewhere I can get the type of cap I need ? James, Danville, PA.

Hello James.

If you remove the brown phenolic strip you could rotate the shaft CCW as desired. However, it is very likely, say 95%, that you'll not get that piece off without distorting any of the rotor blades. You can't turn the cap upside down either, since you'd get the same action of CW begets less capacitance.

There are reversing shafts on the market for large engines but I have never seen a reversing shaft for 1/4-inch shafts. Perhaps you could contrive some sort of gear mechanism? 73, Phil, W0XI

Phil:

Great November news letter. I have two questions : Detector circuit page 9:: how is the 9 volt battery connected to the pick-up/detector circuit shown on page 9.

Can you direct me to a schematic describing a hookup for a MK-484 radio on a chip. I would lie to explore using that as a detector –rf amplifier set up to fee a receiver. Hope to hear back joe winkler

Joe,

I may have not made it clear in the MINI_SQUARE_ LOOP RADIO article that:

I used ten turns for the tuned circuit consisting of C1 ad L2. I then added a single turn and wound it on the same frame in the middle. What happens is the energy in the tuned circuit of C1 and L2 is coupled magnetically into the single turn, L2, which is wired directly to the 1N34 detector.

Second, the MK484 IC/chip was described in detail in the Nov 2012 newsletter.

You can download a pdf file of the MK484 by searching on the internet for MK484 and then print it off. good luck, Phil

Phil,

I have an antenna question another supplier could not answer. I have a small back yard, and I bought a 70 ft / 10 ga uncoated antenna to string.   The problem is that I don't have 70 ft of linear room anywhere, so I had to do an "L" shape, with 20 ft in one direction, 50 ft in the other. I have built two crystal kits so far, one of which is yours.   Both work, but they are pretty weak. I am close to the city, and we have a 50,000 watt AM station here, that I can pick up. So I thought I would buy another 30 - 40 ft, solder it onto the long end of the wire, so now I would have a "Z", but it would be 100+ ft in total length.

The person I asked said that from what he has learned (but he's not sure) that any variance from straight length basically acts as two antennas, not one long one. A "Z" antenna may not add anything onto my total length and increase the volume.

Hello Robert,

Antennas are a bit like cars; there are lots of models and they all work about the same but some have extra features. Generally, one does better for local reception with most of the antenna horizontal and one does better for long distance with most of the antenna vertical (mostly up, perhaps into a tree).

The subject is very broad and also reception depends upon the ionosphere and sunspots, etc. Performance is hard to pinpoint.

To get a better feel for antennas, I would recommend that you buy a copy of the Amateur Radio Handbook from the arrl at www.arrl.org and then read the chapter on antennas.

Hi

Previously I purchased your oat box crystal kit. I just recently purchased your infinite impedance detector kit to improve its performance. Your instruction do not tell you how to connect it to the oat box crystal set. Can you provide that information. Thank you. **Larry Scofield**

Larry, Here's how to connect it. For a typical crystal set – like the Oat Box Set shown in the diagram on the next page – The coil (L1) is wired from point "a" to the input of the 1N34 diode at point "b." In addition the crystal

ear piece attaches across the 47K resistor, labeled R1.

To attach the coil L1 and capacitor C1 to the infinite impedance detector instead, remove the wire going to the diode at "b" and connect it instead to the top connection on the PCB at CONN1. In turn run a ground wire from the bottom of the coil to the bottom connector on the PCB at Connector CONN1. The two connections on the PCB are highlighted in the second picture. Remember to move the leads of the earpiece to conn2 pads on the PCB as noted in the picture.
Enjoy. Phil. Xtal Set Society.

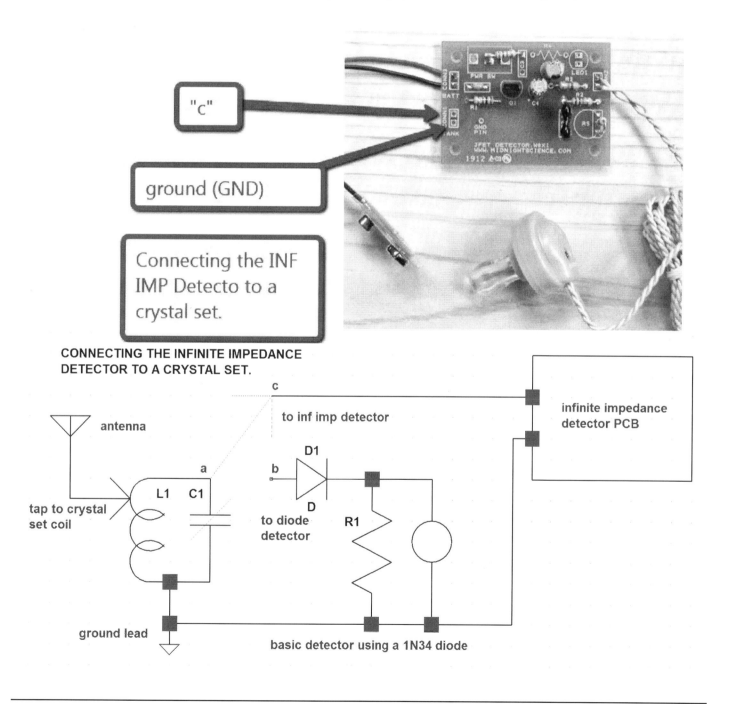

"C"

ground (GND)

Connecting the INF IMP Detecto to a crystal set.

CONNECTING THE INFINITE IMPEDANCE DETECTOR TO A CRYSTAL SET.

c

to inf imp detector

infinite impedance detector PCB

antenna

D1

a

b

L1   C1

D

tap to crystal set coil

to diode detector   R1

ground lead

basic detector using a 1N34 diode

Good evening Patricia,
Please find attached a photo of our Scouts with their completed crystal radios and Morse keys. The project was a lot of hard work but also a lot of fun. Regards, Evan

Hi Folks

Having a lot of 18 AWG copper wire on hand and being bored without many projects to do, would I be wasting my time making a whopper spider coil to use as a directional antenna? I have the lid off a 5 gallon plastic bucket that is a foot across to make the form with, or would I use the Tinker toy type spoke wheel, maybe with 11 spokes?

I'm not expecting much from it, and it'll probably end up as a clever storage spool for the wire. It won't be the first time this happens.

Could a basket weave work for this gizmo? I haven't ever (I think) seen either one used for this purpose, most of them being used for variometer and circuit coils. The basket weave would act more like a loop antenna though. And how about those pancake coils mounted to the inside of early tube portable radio back covers? I don't have one to look at but I assume they were antenna supplements to the telescoping type antennas. John Plante Thanxtel

John. The old loop antennas found on the back of old AM radios are certainly directional. I'd try that one. They act similar to a coil-ferrite rod combination. The spider coil is wound on a flat surface, similar to the old loop antennas wound and mounted on the back of the radio cabinet. You could go that way too. If you have lots of wire, consider winding two loops and then you can couple the antenna loop to the radio loop and adjust their distance and angle to improve selectivity. Phil.

How About Some "Light Listening"
by Dan Petersen, W7OIL

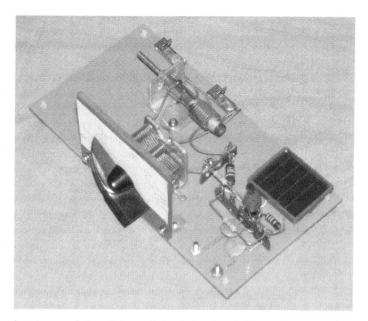

Back in the "good old days", those years "B.C." which of course meant "Before Computers" I, as a young lad, had several radio parts stores and at least a half-dozen "war surplus" stores to blow my allowance in. Telrad Electronics had loopsticks for 39 cents, capacitors and resistors aplenty and even some of the latest GE transistors that came in their own cardboard box like a vacuum tube. I had to save up for a couple of weeks to get a GE-1 transistor - I seem to recall they were over a dollar...ouch! One of the most coveted components was the solar cell. There were two fairly common types, the B2M selenium solar cell and the S1M silicon solar cell, both made by International Rectifier. The B2M was also spendy at a couple of bucks but the S1M, while the price escapes me was enormously expensive, perhaps four dollars. Remember that my weekly allowance was a princely $1.00 a week!

So where does this lead? There was a craze going of radios powered by different items you would not normally associate with power generation. There was the lemon battery, the potato battery, the "Chlorox™" battery and the solar cell. Germanium transistors can operate at less than 1/2 volt so battery efficiency was not paramount. So the radio magazines abounded with articles about novel radios and some of the projects even worked! Fast-forwarding to today I shall now describe a more modern version of the tried and sometimes true sun (or light) powered radio.

Let there be light!
The first order of business is to round up a solar cell. This may be easier than you think. A trip to my local "Dollar Tree™" store was all that was necessary as they had some Christmas-themed LED solar yard lights for, you guessed it, a dollar. Figure 1 illustrates the yard light in all its cheap chinese-manufactured glory. The drum-shaped head is what you should be interested in. It comes off with a mere twist from the clear section. the remainder can be discarded unless you can find a use for something that no longer has a use. The

bottom of the "drum" is detached from the rest by removing two screws (see Figure 2) and carefully pulling it away. There are two wires between the sections so don't do your "Incredible Hulk" impression while doing this. Broken wires, bad Hulk! No cookie!!

Clip the two little wires leading from the solar panel at the little circuit board containing the LED. In Figure 3 the two "X's" show where to cut the wires. As an aside I keep the circuit board and battery as the board can drive a white LED with only 1.2 to 1.5 volts. Now you can go two ways from here; either keep the whole "drum" and mount it to your radio using the two existing screw-holes or carefully cut the solar cell away from the rest of the drum, an example shown in Figure 4. I elected to cut the drum part away but I used great caution - I already sank an "X-acto" knife blade into the palm of my hand once this month. My cell had a green and a white wire. The green wire was "negative" and the White "positive". Also, these are tecnically solar *panels* as they contain more than one *cell*. In full sun these panels put out 3 volts "no-load". The current capability is not great but more than enough for this application.

We Have the Cell, What Now?
The rest of the set is a fairly simple, plain-vanilla one-transistor amplified crystal set. Many of the parts are available from the Xtal Set Society

Figure 1:

Dollar Tree
Solar Yard Light

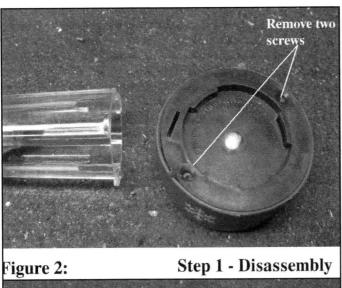

Remove two screws

Figure 2:   **Step 1 - Disassembly**

LED
CIRCUIT
BOARD

SOLAR
CELL

Figure 3:   **The innards**

(http://www.midnightscience.com) including (for a while until they run out) the "loopstick", the variable capacitor, germanium diode and earphone. The transistor, resistors and fixed capacitors are usually found at Radio Shack or on-line. For the article example I used a piece of "Lexan™" plastic sheet for a baseboard. I happened to have all necessary parts ("OILs" junquebox is *well* stocked) including that scarce loopstick. A note of caution, loopsticks are as rare as sneakers for a hippo so if you can get one, fine. Otherwise, you can use a coil with an inductance of around 230 microhenries. A substitute coil can be made from a 3-inch length of 1.5-inch PVC pipe, which an outer diameter of 1.9 inches. Using #24 enameled wire, which the XSS sells, you closewind 84 turns onto the PVC pipe. This will give you a coil of approximately 235 uH inductance.

And Now...the Rest of the Radio.

The schematic in Figure 5 shows the parts in their proper places. You may note that the tuned circuit L1/C1 is not physically wired to the rest of the circuit. It is instead *mutually coupled* to the rest of the circuit. Why is this? Since the antenna is comprised of distributed capacitance and inductance it would have a deliterious effect on the tuned circuit. Tuning is much more selective with this lash-up. You can see that the antenna and ground connections go directly to the link coil L2. Loopsticks usually, when new, have a link coil wound on the outside of the main coil L1 creating a ready-made L2. Connecting the outside world to the link coil minimizes messing up the tuned circuit characteristics. The link coil on the PVC substitute can be made from 6 turns of hookup wire over the center of the coil L1. RF energy is fed to the detector diode, D1, while resistor R1 supplies a load and a DC path for the diode. The detected audio passes through C2 to the base of the transistor Q1. This is shown as a 2N3904 transistor but there are several types that will work as long as they are NPN types. R3 is the collector load resistor. Now a word about biasing the transistor. The voltage on the collector of the transistor referenced to ground should be about 1/2 what the solar cell is producing. This can be adjusted by changing the value of biasing resistor R2. In my case the magic value was 470k ohms. Try that value first. If the collector voltage needs to go up increase the value of R2 and vice-versa. Amplified audio is conducted to the headphones via C3. Resistor R4 is used if a crystal earphone is used. If high-impedance (>2000 ohm) headphones are used R4 is not necessary but it doesn't adversly affect the performance of the radio if it's still there. Figure 6 points out the major placement of the components. Hot-melt glue holds the solar cell to the base.

So Does It Work?
The hacks of the 1950's would claim that a radio like this "Would work forever without batteries!". Well, I guess that would be true if you had an eternal source of light! Personally I think "Fusion Reactor Powered Receiving Apparatus" has a nice ring to it. The sun supplies ALL our energy, directly or indirectly.

After connecting this radio to an antenna and ground Fahnestock (FAWN-stock) clips I connected the crystal earphone across R1 so that I could hear the un-amplified audio from the crock-jocks. As I suspected the set worked pretty much like a good quality crystal radio. The listening was good if you didn't mind two other stations in the background competing for your brain-cells. Now for the acid test!

I connected the crystal earphones to the two 6-32 screws used as terminal posts. Wow! A lot louder. Now the crock-jock on the selected was not only annoying he was yelling his blather into my ears! The other two stations were louder too, making a kind of devil's chorus all jibbering about how they can save the world. I have to say in defense of AM in the Portland/Vancouver area that one station plays oldies music (not the McCarthy hearings thank God-wrong "oldies") for your listening enjoyment. I estimate that the amplification is on the order of 15 decibels or a gain of roughly 30. All this time I was powering the radio from a desk lamp with the bulb about 18 inches from the solar cell. Running it from the desk-lamp proves that not much energy is used. In fact I did a quick calculation. I measured the voltage drop across R3 and found it to be 1.2 volts. Divide that by the resistance (12000 ohms) and you get a current of 100 microamps! Pretty tiny stuff. All in all I found this to be an interesting exercise in innovation and experimentation. I hope you do the same.

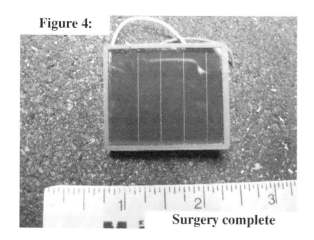

Figure 4:

Surgery complete

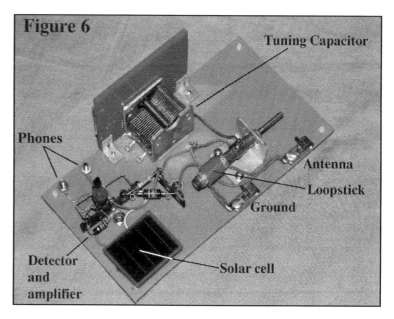

Figure 6

Tuning Capacitor

Phones

Antenna

Loopstick

Ground

Detector and amplifier

Solar cell

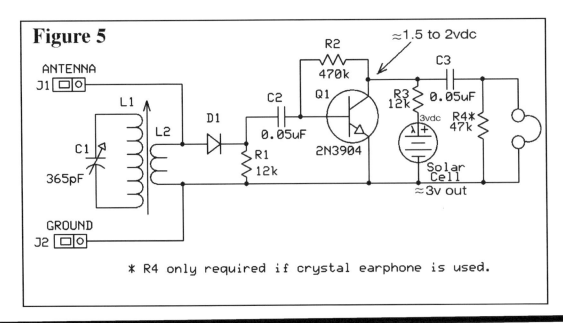

Figure 5

* R4 only required if crystal earphone is used.

Philmore Slider Set: 1940s-1950s
By J.K. Fenton

The Philmore Slider Set as shown in Picture 1 became available in the 1940-1950 era. It is a simple set with a limited number of parts. Phone leads attach to the Fahnestock clips at the upper left; a long-wire antenna attaches to the upper-right clip and system ground to the lower right clip. The Galena detector with cat-whisker is shown at the top. One tunes the station with the slider shown at the bottom.

The various parts are wired together on the back side as shown in Picture 2 with metal strips. Thus the set required no soldering. At close inspection, one can see that the coil, wound on a piece of wood, has only one connection to the antenna terminal via a screw to the antenna Fahnestock clip. The other connection is made at the bottom of the slider through the rounded opening on the front panel. Given that this is the only variable part in the set, the slider tunes the frequency of reception.

ABOUT THE COIL
The wooden coil form is 3 by 1.75 by 0.4 inches. The coil is centered longwise on the form and has 210 turns of 10 mil enameled wire. I estimated the inductance of the coil by equating the area of the opening at the end of the wooden form with that of a cylindrical coil.

Hence,

$$a*b = \pi r^2, \text{ so rearranging, } r = \sqrt{\frac{a*b}{\pi}}$$

$$\text{so } r = \sqrt{\frac{1.75*0.4}{\pi}} = 0.45 \text{ inches.}$$

Using Wheeler's equation for a cylindrical coil with a radius of 0.5, 210 turns and a pitch of 0.012 inches, the inductance is roughly 371 uH (micro-Henry). I used about 2/3 of the coil to tune in KLWN at 1320 kHz. That seems about right. Keep in mind that the length of your antenna with determine the capacitance of the tuned circuit.

I've drawn the set schematic. Any antenna – usually 40 to 50 feet of wire – for the AM band is short compared to the wavelength of the radio waves in the AM band; hence, the impedance of the antenna is capacitive and labeled C-ANT. This capacitance and the slider coil make up the tuned circuit for the set. One adjusts the position of the slider to tune the radio to a desired frequency. The galena and rock detector converts the AM radio signal to audio; and, the earpiece produces the audio sound.

It is likely that the crystal ear pieces used in sets today

were not available in 1950. Radio hams and short-wave listeners of the time used coil-based headphones. One common brand was Baldwin. The DC impedance of most of those old phones was about 2,000 ohms with an AC impedance of about 10K ohms. These phone, of course are hard to find today. Most sets today make use of cheap crystal ear piece. The ear piece is nothing more than a disc shaped capacitor with one side being a thin metal disk and the other side (of the capacitor) an insulated deposited disc of conducting material. As such it is necessary to add a 47k to 100k resistor in parallel with the ear piece to produce audio.

I operated the set with my 40 to 50 foot attic antenna and received our local 500 watt AM station, KLWN, at 1320 kHz readily. My bench ground has earth ground, obtained from a rod just a few feet outside the window. I did not check the DX performance of this set – i.e. long distance operation. Since the Q of the wooden based coil is moderate one would not expect high performance with the set. But keep in mind, this was a very inexpensive set for its time and likely enjoyed by millions! These sets can still be found for sale via the internet.

Picture 1

Picture 2

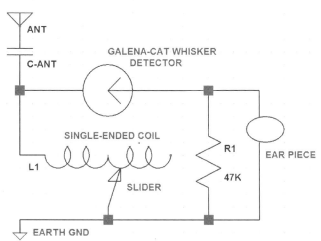

Finding A Suitable Cabinet For Your Home Built Radio
By Bob Helt

One of the most difficult things most home builders encounter is what to do with that working radio chassis with the exposed tuning capacitor to make it look more finished and professionally appearing. It seems like friends and family are a lot less impressed by how well your radio works rather than how it looks. Face it, the bare chassis with exposed tuning capacitor and unbaffled speaker just doesn't impress most folks. It may work great but so many others judge a radio on how it looks as well as how it performs.

Faced with this problem for many years, I tried many solutions. First was attempting to use several different wooden boxes I located from various sources. Well the boxes did hide the circuit components, but the result still looked amateurish and unfinished. Then I attempted to fit the radio into a purchased Plastic enclosure. This allowed the radios to be more finished looking but still there was that appearance of being unprofessional and obviously home built.

Finally a suggestion on the internet pointed me to the perfect solution. And it may also be a perfect one for you too no matter whether your radio is a simple crystal set or a more complicated TRF or superhet circuit.

The Perfect Solution

What is this "perfect solution"? It is to use a TIVOLI radio cabinet, gut the interior components and install your radio circuit in its place. What the heck is a Tivoli radio and how might one get one you might ask? The Tivoli was the brilliant design of engineer Henry Kloss of KLH, Inc. fame. He designed not only the electronics that to me seem less spectacular, he also designed the audio cabinetry, and his company has sold them starting around the year 2000 to the present day.

Tivoli Audio offers a wide variety of radios so what you want is specifically a Model One, the basic unit. In addition you should know that there are two versions of the Model One Tivoli. Either one will do for our purposes but you should know just what you are getting. The first version of the Model One has a three position selector switch for Off, FM, and AM. The second version includes these three positions, but adds another switch position for an AUX input. This has importance to us only because of the markings on the front panel and how we will use them.

This is a Tivoli model one, except that the knobs have been replaced to match the builder's desires. Note how the tuning knob fits exactly into the original space.

The Tivoli radio, Model One, offers a superb wooden cabinet measuring approx 8"X5"X5" that will accommodate most any home built radio. Then it is an audio marvel producing a rich sound that to many people rivals the Bose radio system. The secret of this outstanding sound producer lies in the cabinet design, bass port and wide-range 5-watt loud speaker, all of which can be retained and used for the home builder's radio. So to start with the basic cabinet with bass port and speaker offers one the perfect choice of a neat looking cabinet with an attractive wooden finish and a professional appearance that is so illusive, plus an unrivaled sound. The Front panel of the Tivoli can also be completely integrated in to the home builder's plans too.

How to get a Tivoli radio

OK, here's the big secret, both new and used Tivoli radios are sold and bought on Ebay. Just go on Ebay and look for Tivoli Radios (Or Google Tivoli radio and see what is currently offered). Now, new Tivolis are fairly expensive so what you want is a used one, preferable a NON-Working one, since you intend to remove the electronics anyhow. A little known fact is that The Tivoli Audio Company has DECLINED to make public a circuit diagram of their radios. That means that "no one" knows how to repair a non-working unit. Maybe some people can swap working components for failed ones cannibalizing other Tivoli radios but basically a non-working unit can't be repaired. And to complicate that situation, apparently the Tivoli Audio Company doesn't repair failed radios outside of their 2-year warranty either. After their two year warranty expires, they just offer new replacements at a reduced price. It would appear that this inability to repair Tivoli radios aftermarket creates a fairly significant flow of these failed units onto the market for our benefit. So the best thing is to search out a non-working one that can be bought cheaply on Ebay. If you do acquire a working Tivoli radio and don't intend to keep it as an original Tivoli, you might possibly be able to remove the working components and sell them on Ebay.

Yes, even used, the Tivoli radios are not cheap but let's consider the VALUE you are getting for your money. A well made, solid wood sided, acoustical chamber, designed to enhance the sounds emitted from the electronics inside (and yours too). This is with a high quality 3" speaker included. And maybe most important to us, is the very easy conversion to house most any air-variable tuned home-built radio circuit.

Removing the Old Electronics

The first step is removing the knobs. These are just push-on knobs and no set screws are involved. So wrap masking tape around each knob allowing a length of tape to grab onto and pull. If the tape comes off before the knob, repeat the operation.

Next is to remove the four Philips-head screws located at the corners at the back. Follow this up by removing the two recessed Philips screws at the near center of the back panel. Do not remove any other screws at this time. Now the fun part is pulling out the front panel toward the front and the back panel out the back. These two panels are just a tight fit in the enclosure. Nothing is holding them in place now except friction. So work both of them loose. Don't unplug any cables now.

You can now lay the back panel flat and slide it toward the front panel and remove both panels together from the front of the cabinet. Now unplug the speaker wire.

Remove the front dial, vernier and tuner box from the front panel. Remove the rest of the components from the front panel including the PCB. Remove the components from the back panel. Both the front and rear panels will now be clean. Keep everything you removed all connected together in case you may want to use it in the future or maybe sell it.

Parts to retain or replace

You want to retain the following parts: Cabinet, Bare rear panel, Bare front panel, Tuning dial, Possibly the tuning knob, All screws and hardware

The following are the specialty parts you want to procure to make this a simple and easily conversion:

A Planetary Reduction Drive (tuning vernier) from The Xtal Set Society (https://www.midnightscience.com/index.html).

A front mount air-variable tuning capacitor (VC), either single ganged or dual ganged to suit your needs. These capacitors will have threaded holes on the front side (where the shaft is) for front mounting. Both Single and dual ganged VCs are available from the Xtal Set Society (https://www.mid-nightscience.com/index.html).

In addition a dual ganged VC (ALPS brand) with two different max capacitances is available on the Internet. Google Alps VC and check Ebay). Also see <http://www.ebay.com/itm/ALPS-Air-Variable-Capacitor-20-320pf-for-Crystal-Radio-Antenna-Tuner-Ham-Radio-/141381697550?pt=LH_Def aultDomain_0&hash=item20eb01800e> There are other sources too.

A 4"X4" piece of 1/8" thick polystyrene sheet or equivalent to mount the VC to.

Assembly of the specialty parts

Start with the front panel. The new vernier will bolt right in, in place of the old one. So will, the front dial. The tuning knob will not be a direct fit and should be replaced with a purchased one that will fit in the space of the oil one.

A view of the mounted ALPS dual ganged tuning capacitor. The white platform below the VC is not part of this installation but is the bottom of a proto board, part of the builder's circuits.

Trim the polystyrene platform to fit over the three tall mounts (or shafts) surrounding the input to the vernier. Remove the poly platform and carefully drill holes in the poly piece to allow the VC to be front-mounted to it, with the VC shaft aligning with and able to couple to the vernier. Drill holes in the polystyrene platform to align it to these three mounts. Install screws to mount the poly platform with the VC already installed to these three mounts.

A close-up shot of the VC's mounting on the poly platform and the coupling to the vernier.

Finishing the radio

OK, you now have your tuning capacitor mounted and ready to go, along with your speaker. So the rest is up to you. Mount your radio on the two panels and use the two front holes for rotary selector switches, potentiometers, or other controls. You have a lot of opportunities here to build and install so many different circuits and have them all look so good and professional in the Tivoli cabinet.

And as an added note: a little furniture polish will make that wood cabinet shine like it was brand new.

Installing Xtal Set Antenna and Other Station Parts

By Chip, W7AIT

My next-door neighbor installed my Xtal set society, "50 foot long wire" and 4 foot earth ground rod today. It's not very high, 10 feet and below roof line but it works great! Really pulls in the BBC stations on crystal sets!

The first set I tested was my JFET infinite impedance detector set (modified lm386 audio amplifier and speaker), then my Heathkit cr-1 (copy of the famous Heathkit cr-1 crystal set of 1955 through 1961) with external Pebbles lm386 audio amplifier. The Peebles amplifier was highly modified by me with 2n2222a transistor preamplifier and now has a selectable gain of 200 or 18,000.

Picture 1: "mid point" of 50 foot antenna wire.

Picture 2: End of Antenna. Note Twist

This antenna is for receiving only, not for transmitting, therefore has no lightening protection features.

I may add a kelvin plate later. I could also neaten up antenna and ground lead in wiring.

A simple wire antenna like this is all it takes to get reasonable performance from crystal sets.

I'll run nighttime testing and see if I can pull in night DX say from KTNN NAVAHO NATION in Window Rack AZ on the New Mexico border, KSL in Salt Lake UT, and KOMO in Seattle.

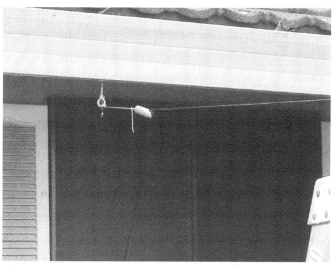

Picture 3: shack end of antenna, strain relief, and loose feedline, headed for shack.

Picture 4: connected to jfet set.

Picture 5: jfet set close up.

Picture 6: xtal ground rod and line

Bill Holly
Most creative with the box

Hi, Here's my entry for the cigar box xtal set contest. The circuit is from "50 Tested Wireless Circuits" Edited by F.J. Camm circa 1930. I omitted the switchable loading coil he showed in the circuit but otherwise it's the same. The circuit is similar to Alan Klase's "Pretty Good Xtal Set" shown on his website. The circuit is very sensitive and by

adjusting the detector and antenna feed points you can achieve a fair amount of selectivity but if you are in a crowed RF environment you would benefit from the use of one or more traps. This circuit would probably be much more satisfactory in a more rural location. Hi Q parts and wire probably would have helped considerably. I used ten taps and the top tap switch is the antenna and the bottom switch is for the detector. The capacitor is an el cheepo slf variable of about 400pf. The coil is #22 awg solid plastic insulated wire wound in a one over one under pattern on a five in. diameter form made with 3/4 inch plywood and 20 penny nails. All crosses are held with hot melt glue. The coil is 249 mh. The "Professor Morse" label is a scanned copy of

my original printed on sticky back label and covered with a plastic laminate sheet. Made it hard to get a good photo without a glare spot. The overall size of the box is 7 1/4 inch by 9 1/8 inch by 3 1/8 inch deep and the interior is 6 1/8 inch by 8 1/2 inch by 2 1/2 inch deep. The front panel is 3/16 micarta that I sanded down with a palm sander to get a mat finish and is mounted on two pieces of 1/2 inch thick pine. It slides into the box with a snug fit but is easily removeable for service or exhibition. With the lid closed there's about a sheet of paper thickness over the knobs so the set doesn't rattle or "bang" around when moving it about. The box originally held fifty "House of Windsor" cigars made in Windsor, PA. I Thought the "Professor Morse" label would be more appropriate for a cigar box radio and it was a perfect

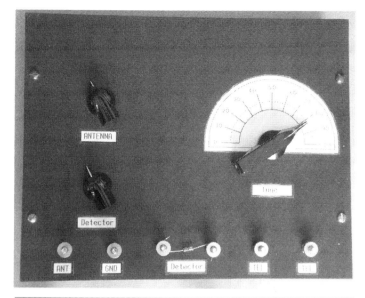

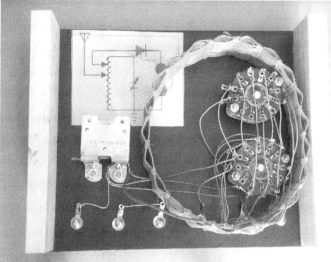

A bit of nostalgia from a Johnson Smith & CO catalog. Can anyone explain the War-Developed Diode?

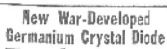

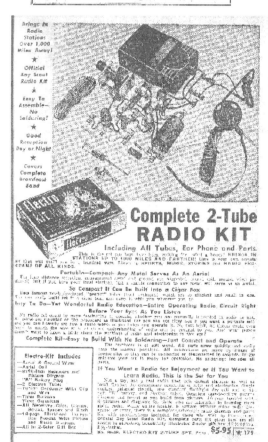

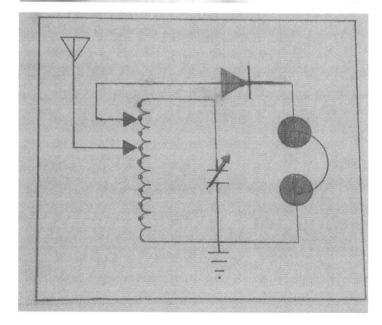

Larry Jeffers
Most complex Design

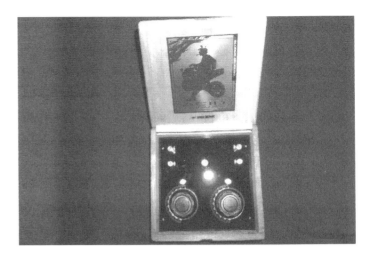

The society asked for Crystal sets built in cigar boxes. I went looking and came up with a nice box. Now the fun begins! How to fill it with a set that looks great and also has good performance.

I had two nice vernier capacitors and Litz wire, so now the fun starts.

The box has a flush lid, so it would need a recessed panel. After a few measurements and a couple days of thinking, I got started. First some rails to mount the panel at a depth that would leave clearance for the knobs and dials were glued in place and a panel was cut to fit. Then some brass parts were made including hubs to put the dials on capacitors, end fed, binding posts and pointer markers for the dials. Then the coil mounting and coils were made and everything mounted and wired.

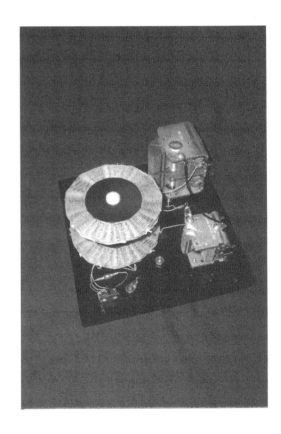

This set performs beautifully! I get 10 daytime stations which is great for my area. We have one local station at 5 miles and one at 45 miles. All others are 60- 180 miles away. At night it really comes to life. It is selective and loud. The dials track well, peaking within 1 or 2 points. The antenna section is fairly broad tuning and may not need a vernier. The detector section tunes very sharp.

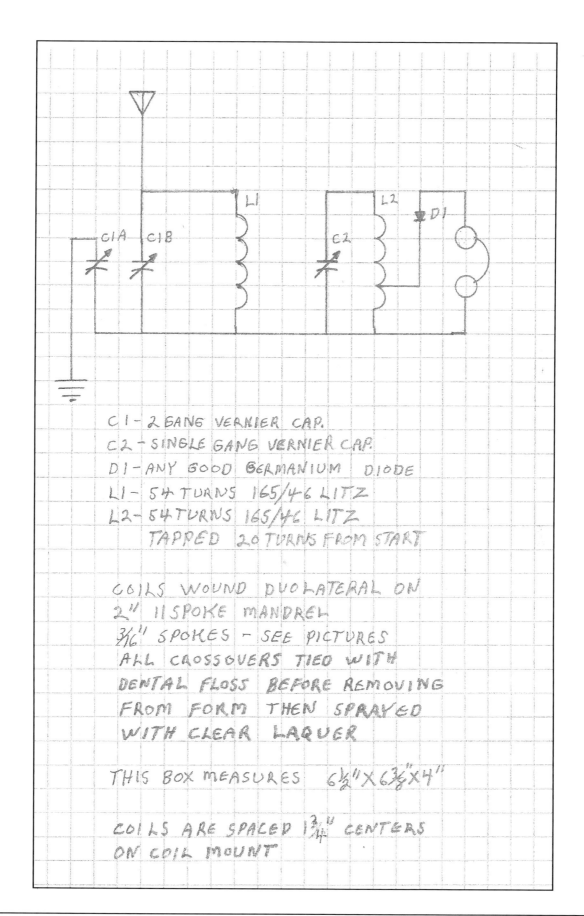

C1 - 2 GANG VERNIER CAP.

C2 - SINGLE GANG VERNIER CAP.

D1 - ANY GOOD GERMANIUM DIODE

L1 - 54 TURNS 165/46 LITZ

L2 - 54 TURNS 165/46 LITZ
        TAPPED 20 TURNS FROM START

COILS WOUND DUOLATERAL ON
2" 11 SPOKE MANDREL
3/16" SPOKES - SEE PICTURES
ALL CROSSOVERS TIED WITH
DENTAL FLOSS BEFORE REMOVING
FROM FORM THEN SPRAYED
WITH CLEAR LAQUER

THIS BOX MEASURES 6½"X 6⅜"X 4"

COILS ARE SPACED 1¾" CENTERS
ON COIL MOUNT

Chip Olheiser
Most complete Documentation

I saw the November Newsletter and the contest announcement. This was a challenge because as simple as some crystal sets are, it can be difficult to package them in a given, defined footprint.

My style of building homebrew is to provide enough documentation to be able to repair it later; usually a schematic and parts list is all that's required. But this contest has the requirement of bounding the physical dimensions inside a box - or it could have been built outside the box on its outer surfaces but that just didn't seem right to me - and providing documentation sufficient to "show it off".

My original design starts with a schematic draft, then a working breadboard prototype; this process may be repeated multiple times. Then I work to finalize the design down to an acceptable final parts list and schematic. The parts list step is absolutely critical because I don't know what to buy to build the working unit until I know what parts I need to purchase. Procurement of deliverable hardware parts is thus held up until the prototype design is completely working and meeting all design requirements.

Part of this process is to "Muntzify" the design. "Muntzification" comes from the TV set manufacturer Earl William "Madman" Muntz. What he'd do is take a TV set design and start pulling parts out until the TV set stopped working, put that last part back in and then sell that design in his TV set manufacturing factories -cheap! Cheap because he got all the excessive cost out by pulling parts!

I did the same thing. My original design had all sorts of circuits including Shocktty Barrier Diode detector, LITZ wire coils, built in audio amplifier, speaker and a internal battery pack.

But then the issue of the Cigar Box popped up. I'd found a beautiful, old Cigar Box that I'd bought back in 1977 but the design had too many parts to fit in the box! Besides, that box has a history! More on that in a minute. But the Cigar Box was available. But how to fit my design inside the box? Before I answer that, here's the brief history of that Cigar Box.

Cigar box history: I bought the Cigar Box back in 1977 at Eastridge Mall in San Jose, CA. I used to smoke cigars back then. The Casa Cuba cigars were excellent, great mellow taste and smoke; I smoked them all. They were about $1.60 each - at today's prices that's probably a $6 cigar. But these were very excelled, high quality cigars.

I even took that box with me on a business trip to Atlanta Georgia (Warner Robbins Air Force Base). I'd smoke a cigar in the evenings and my company coworker travelling companions saw the Casa Cuba label, thought that I'd flipped over to Castro Communist party! Nah, they were just joking. Anyway, very excellent cigars indeed.

The box was then storage for a DMM I'd bought at a flea market. It was storage for about 20 years. The box survived 6 or 7 moves until it ended up here in Modesto. It sat empty here for another 10 years until 2 months ago when I decided to use it for this competition. So now its turned into a Crystal Radio Set! What a history.

Needless to say, the biased Shocktty Diodes, built in audio amplifier, speaker, and battery pack all were removed. The coil still was a major issue. To lay flat, I chose a Spider coil form. Coils L1 and L2 were designed using 150/46/ served LITZ wire and RF swept bench tested for maximum tuning range, the target being 540 to 1705 kHz. Also, tried for maximum detector voltage output and minimum MDS (minimum discernable signal). I also tested for 1N34A detector damage as I have some nearby high power amateur transmitters

---

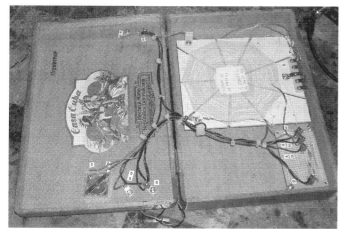

and antennas in close proximity to my SWL crystal set antennas. All passed.

The one big problem though, is tuning band rejection or the ability to pull weak stations out near the local "Flame Thrower" 50,000 watt local stations. Modesto is blessed with 2 of these Flame Throwers. No matter what I tired with coil "Q", capacitor "Q", and RF grounding, I cannot successfully reject 100% of these Flame Thrower signals all of the time. What saves me is at night, these stations are required by FCC to lower the power from 50,000 watts to 4,100 watts in one case and 4,000 watts to 950 watts in the second case. The third switches antenna pattern so its lobes switch at night time.

Note that my design has user selectable inductance "Tweak" taps. This is to allow for variation of capacitive reactance of the antennas - user selects tap for best

performance with his antenna. That way, tuning range is basically preserved as well as MDS.

I had fun testing this set as I used swept RF testing techniques to see the actual frequency response of the tuned circuits over the entire band. I rarely get the opportunity to sweep design circuits and this set was perfect for that kind of real time testing and tweaking. I was able to get things just right.

By the way, measured performance is MDS -37 dbm, tuning range of 495 to 1470 kHz, 3 db stop band tuning bandwidth is 116 kHz, and a typical output voltage preamplification of 108 MVPP. The 1N34A was successfully tested to burnout level of 20 volts Vr. I did not test 1N34A If burnout as its 500 milliamps and I have no signals that would drive the diode that hard, so the test is unnecessary.

The capacitor audio output terminal drives the amplifier best with gain set to 18,000X, though the "Flame Thrower" stations will drive the audio amplifier at gain set to 200X.

Addendum:

I measured the Peebles PO-386 with mods using precision step attenuators, Spectrum Analyzer and Tracking Generator. I swept from 10 kHz to 30 kHz. This produced the following gains: PO-386 has a gain of 47 db on the high setting. Its gain on low setting is only 8 db.

The combined Cigar Crystal set, and now the PO-386 gain set to HIGH, produces a new MDS of about -82 dbm or a S7 signal. The combined total, end to end of the entire set, will detect AM stations

to -82 dbm or about S7 level signals.

This explains its ability to pick up weak, distant DX stations at night.

Anyway I had fun building this project and even more fun measuring and characterizing the set using modern test equipment and test techniques. It explains exactly what is going on and what to expect. A very fun, enjoyable project indeed.

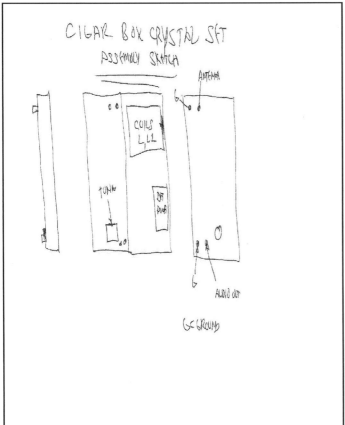

CIGAR BOX CRYSTAL SET PARTS LIST

TOP ASSEMBLY
LONG WIRE ANTENNA
CIGAR BOX CRYSTAL SET
PEEBLES AUDIO AMPLIFIER
TWISTED PAIR WIRE 6 FEET

SUBASSEMBLIES, A2
COIL SUBASSEMBLY L1, L2
COIL FORM, SPIDER COIL XTAL SET SOCIETY
LITZ WIRE, 100 FOOT ROLL XTAL SET SOCIETY

DIODE DETECTOR SUBASSEMBLY
0.1 UF CAP 50 V C2
1N34A DIODE D1
47 K OHM, 1/4 WATT CARBON RESISTOR
INDUCTOR, 33 UH L4
INDUCTOR, 82 UH L3
INDUCTOR, 47 UH L5
RADIO SHACK PWB A9
TERMINALS, SCREW

SUBASSEMBLY CIGAR BOX

BINDER POST 4
CASA CUBA CIGAR BOX, 7X10X2
CLEAR VARNISH PAINT
HOOK UP WIRE STRANDED 26 AWG, WHITE
MISC. HARDWARE, STANDOFFS
RUBBER FEET 4
TUNING CAPACITOR PEEBLES PHILMORE 1951

SUBASSEMBLY TWISTED PAIR WIRES
TWISTED PAIR WIRE 6 FEET 2A 4

USER PROVIDED ANTENNA, AUDIO AMPLIFIER

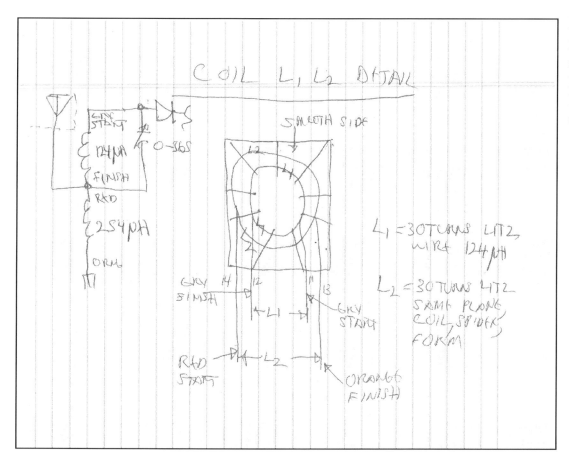

COIL L₁ L₂ DETAIL

SMOOTH SIDE

L_1 = 30 TURNS LITZ WIRE 124 μH

L_2 = 30 TURNS LITZ SAME PLANE COIL SPIDER FORM

Editor: Chip sent many more graphs and charts showing his measurements. Lots of really good detail.

Anthony L Dunn
Use of the catwhisker

My finished entry for the Cigar Box Radio contest is a double-tuned, mutually resonant circuit, with an extra variable capacitor for antenna tuning. I have it set up to work with either a catwhisker detector or a diode, depending on my mood. The box you sent was so nice I decided not to drill any holes in it, but instead built my radio on a piece of ash plywood stained to match the box and mounted on four corner blocks glued inside my box. My variable capacitors are mounted on two homemade copper spacer plates, with extensions to reach my antenna and ground binding posts. The knobs are actually wooden drawer pulls, stained and fitted with brass setscrews. My dials are cut out of the same plywood as the chassis board. There is an extra 220pf

capacitor not shown on the schematic, which is across the antenna tuning cap to give the desired range.

I'm having a ball playing with this, now that it's complete. It is very selective and fairly sensitive (with 75 feet of antenna) and I can get 8 stations at night with it. I guess I'm hooked on the Xtal radio hobby!

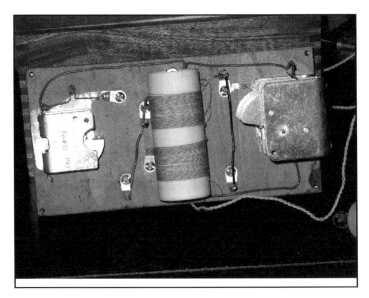

Anthony's Xtal Set

C1, C2, C3, 365pf air variable
C1 & C2 ganged
C4 100pf
C5 500pf
R1 47K
D1 Galena or Pyrite, provisions to subst. 1n34a

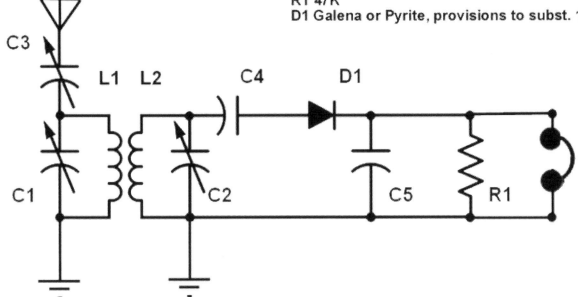

L1, L2 are both 62 turns 20/44 Litz on 1-1/4 pvc form. Contra-wound, in phase.
Will probably try Bogen T725 in place of R1.

Using A Transistor To Boost Crystal Set Gain/output

By Phil, WØXI.

Carl, from Connecticut, sent me a scan of a page about an old article in Electronics Digest titled "Gernsback Interflex Receiver." His interest is in using a transistor to boost the gain of a crystal set. The article page included both transistor and tube version schematics.

I've redrawn the transistor version, which is shown in Figure 2, using my circuit simulation program from LT Spice. However, to check out the circuit, I also pulled up a previous circuit, shown in Figure 1 that verifies/shows how the basic diode detector crystal set works. Let's examine that circuit first.

The generator shown in figure 1 as V1, simulates the voltage generated by the tuning coil in an actual circuit. I used a 1N914 diode here since I don't have a model in the program for the usual 1N34 germanium. However, that doesn't matter since we are not trying to optimize the circuit, just see how it works. R2 represents the hi-z headphones and C1 shows the usual RF bypass capacitor.

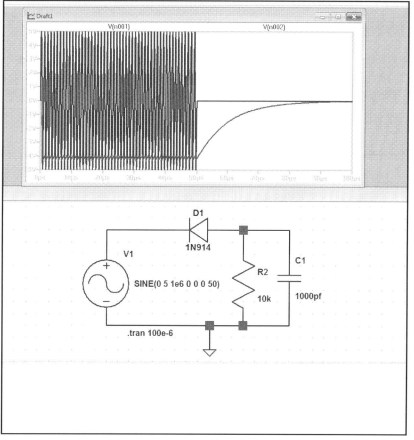

I set the program to generate a 50 microsecond burst of a 1 MHz carrier; that signal is shown in the graph above the circuit. Note that the voltage at the output of the diode, across R2, immediately drops to about -4 volts as the signal is applied, as expected. Then, when the pulse of RF energy stops, the diode no longer conducts and the charge dissipates from C1 to R2 at the output, thus following roughly the input signal. That's what a crystal set does.

Now let's look at Figure 2, which shows the simulation when the transistor, a 2N2907, is added to the circuit along with the needed battery.

Note that the positive side of the battery is tied to ground along with the emitter of the PNP transistor. That forces the DC voltage at the collector to be -3 volts. Now let's see what happens as the radio frequency voltage is applied to the circuit. As the signal voltage swings negative, that forward biases the transistor and diode and current flows through the transistor from emitter to collector. That Current also flows through R2, our simulated headphones and then returns to the battery. Note in the signal plot at the top of the figure that the voltage at the collector started at -3 VDC (at the far left) and then jumps up to 0 and that after the radio signal was removed (at the middle of the graph) the output voltage slowly drops back to its starting voltage of -3 volts. That would indicate that the output of the circuit is a replica of the peak value of the signal voltage. Houston, "we have lift off." The circuit seems to be working.

I've not wired up a set on the bench and run this circuit for real. I'll try to find the time to do that before the next newsletter deadline. If you try this circuit too, let us know how you did. Note that we did not try to optimize the above circuit; we just wanted to verify that it works about the same as the diode only circuit.

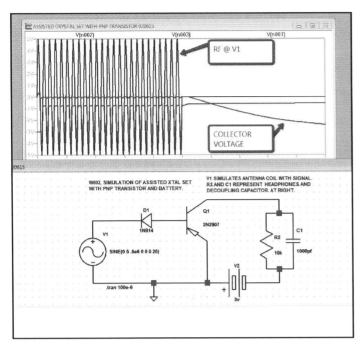

Figure 2

Musings From a Long Winter
by Dan Petersen - W7OIL

As I write this the signs of spring are popping up everywhere. The daffodils have been daffing, the tulips are tuling and the clematis is - clemming(?). I won't mention what the bleeding heart plant is doing! The streets are wet (In the Northwest? DUH!) but winter is losing its grip. I read where things were, um, snowy in the Northeast. One report said the rescue services are hoping to get snow removal gear into downtown Boston by July. The fire departments had to chip the dogs away from the fire hydrants before they could fight a fire. Well, not THAT bad but the word "snow" makes north-easterners turn funny colors right now. On the other hand, they had to truck snow IN for the Alaska Iditarod race. And now it's "Climate Change" because the eco-goons find it hard to say "Global Warming" when they are standing armpit deep in snow. Go figure.

So what does this have to do with crystal sets? Well...how about ANTENNA SEASON! Three years ago I moved from radio Nirvana to radio Purgatory, acreage to a nice retirement village with antenna restrictions and "postage stamp" lots. Radio Nirvana had such a low man-made noise level and acreage that I could hear atmospheric noise on a crystal set with NO amplification using my "RMS Titanic" antenna. Now in the Urban Jungle I am lucky to hear myself think with all the TV's, light dimmers, 279,623 switching power supplies for laptops and other sundry necessities of life these days. No outside antennas. I do however, have a flagpole in the back "yard" (allowable) that by some fantastic coincidence is resonant at the 20 meter ham band. I also have snuck a 60-foot wire antenna up along the ridge of the roof. The 40-meter loop (experimental) in the sun-porch will not be discussed here. The wire antenna across the roofline has an associated ground rod right outside my man-cave. It is this antenna that I wish to center my discussion around.

Knowing the restrictions of my wire antenna I have tried to maximize every aspect of its design.

I then wished to determine the parameters of the antenna for maximum efficiency.

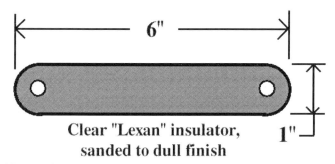

Clear "Lexan" insulator, sanded to dull finish

Figure 1

Maximize the Situation, Minimize the Visibility

There are a few rules-of-thumb that can apply here. Longer is better, higher is better and longer AND higher is best. Now I have to hide my clandestine operations from whom I call the "Yard-Nazis". In grade-school these finks were called "tattle-tales", those kids that would sell you down the river for the chance to feel smug. The yard-nazis haven't grown up since grade-school. Every "Geezer Farm" (retirement community) has at least one mated pair of yard-nazis. So the antenna has to be as non-visible as possible. I used #22 stranded wire with a white teflon insulation. Why teflon? Because I had a big roll of it. Insulators can be a problem as they can be seen fairly easily. Use clear "Lexan" and sand it dull so it will not flash in the sunlight. It also transmits light from whatever color is behind it. See Figure 1. Grey in this climate is a good camouflage. My weather station anemometer and wind-vane on the peak of the roof are painted flat grey and I have had no complaints. Placing the antenna supports so that the antenna is about a foot above the shingles and about two feet down from the peak of the roof. This way the wire blends in with the roof and is not silhouetted against the sky. Figure 2 shows basically the arrangement. The lead-in I use is a piece of #8 bare copper wire bent so it bends around the roof and to the porcelain feed-through in the outside wall. When asked about it I tell them it is my "lightning protection" which is not far from the truth. I do keep the antenna grounded when not in use. So now I have an antenna that 90% of experimenters can expect to put up.

Uh, oh – Time to get Technical

In determining the basic parameters you need to make measurements of the antenna resonance and reactance. Both of these parameters can be found with a grid-dip oscillator (GDO) and some mathematics. You can get an idea of the antenna resonance by adding the antenna plus

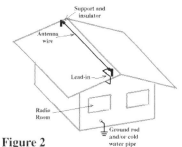

Figure 2

the lead-in length in feet and dividing 234 by the combined antenna and lead-in length. In my case the Aw+Li=62 feet. Plug that into the equation and I get a resonance of 3.77 MHz. Now I take the grid-dip oscillator, wrap a couple of turns around the sensor coil and connect the alligator clips to antenna and ground. I plugged in the appropriate coil and tuned the GDO. Voila! Resonance at 3.91 MHz. Comparing the two means it's "close enough for government work". Since we want to use the antenna (usually) at Broadcast Band frequencies (540-1700 KHz) we now know that the reactance is capacitive – it "looks" like a capacitor. So to tune the antenna to BCB resonance we need to add an inductance. OK – give it my best WAG (wild agreeable guess) and use a crystal set inductor. The one I used has an inductance of 243 microhenries (uH). But wait! There's more!! Large value inductances, especially solenoid-wound ones have a distributed capacitance. At

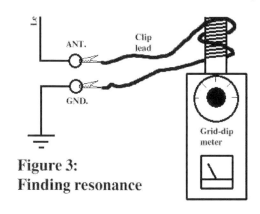

Figure 3: Finding resonance

some point in the spectrum they will resonate all by themselves. This can be found with the trusty GDO – loosely couple the GDO to the coil and search for a resonance (a "dip"). Voila again! This coil resonates at 5.5 MHz. I used a spreadsheet I call "Professor Coyle" to determine the capacitance having a known inductance. The capacitance comes out to 3.7 picofarads (pF). Not very much but still one to keep an eye on.

To determine the capacitance of the antenna, at least in the frequency range of interest consult Figure 4 for details. Now as I look for a resonance I finally find one at 860 KHz. Professor Coyle tells me that the total capacitance at Cn is 152 pF. Subtracting that pesky self resonant capacitance of 3.7 pF I get 147.3 pF, giving me the capacitance, at least at that frequency. This 860 KHz reading is familiar to me. I have a 50kw flame-thrower at 860 KHz about 7 miles from here. What would happen if I connected the coil across the antenna and hitched a diode detector and headphone to it? I connected the coil to the antenna and ground, connected a 1N5711 schottky diode to the antenna side and a pair of 4800 ohm magnetic headphones to the other side of the diode and ground. Result? KPAM-860 roars in like a Kansas tornado. The antenna "Cn" in cahoots with the inductor tune in the crock-jocks very well. I can hear a couple other stations faintly in the background. Note: A modern schottky diode like the 1N5711 is at least as good as the tried and true germanium diode such as the 1N34. You can see in Figure 4 that I also tried a catwhisker detector with an Australian "Brakunga" iron pyrite. Note the neat layout of the receiver. Don't be jealous! Listening to a single talk station would be great if I wanted to listen to verbal bovine fertilizer 24/7. The idea here is to resonate that skyhook on the roof. If we are going to make an inductor that will resonate from 530 to 1700 KHz the math tells us that we need an inductor with a range of 613 uH at 530 KHz to 60 uH at 1700KHz. Quite a spread.

The Loading Coil

Calculations by Professor Coyle indicate that a piece of 4" PVC pipe 5" in length with 88 turns of #18 enameled wire (97 feet) will give me a coil

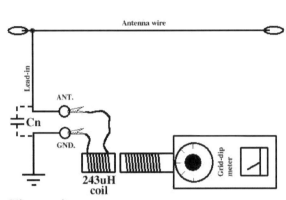

Figure 4:
Antenna capacitance

of 628 uH. I am using a large diameter wire to reduce distributed capacitance. I plan to make it in the fashion of a "slider" coil with a sliding tap. The intent is to make a "loose coupler" set of coils with the crystal set tuning coil movable inside the loading coil.

I ran out of #18 wire at 77 turns. Professor Coyle tells me that the inductance will be 524 uH. I measured it with a precision 300pF capacitor in parallel and GDO dipped it at 403 KHz. Inductance? 527 uH! The "Prof" is usually really close. So how close was I with the coil connected to the antenna? Supposing the antenna capacitance is 147 pF and the coil is 527 uH with a distributed capacitance of 4.2 pF. The Prof says 560 KHz. The GDO dipped it at 570 KHz!

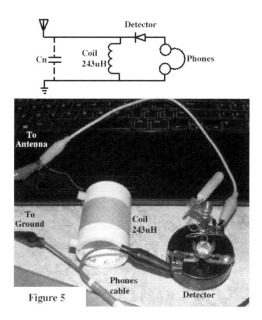

Figure 5

Future Plans

I plan to build a slider onto this coil so I can set the inductance depending on the frequency. Then I will build a crystal set that will couple to the antenna tuning coil via a loose coupler arrangement. Now I do not believe I have ever left my reader dangling at the end of an article but the plans I have will easily fill another article. So stay tuned!

So, who or what is this "Professor Coyle"? "He" is an Excel spreadsheet that aids in coil calculations and other pesky mathematical problems. I designed it about 2003 or so and it has been a godsend. There is also an HTML version at *http://www.crystalradio.net*. Darryl Boyd was kind enough to convert it to HTML. I can send you the latest spreadsheet version via email.
Keep experimenting!
  email: *dan.w7oil@gmail.comv*

A Really Big Crystal Radio
by Stan Kaplan, WB9RQR and Bill Howe, KA9WRL

A few years ago, one of us (Bill Howe) ran across an interesting radio cabinet at a yard sale in Grafton, Wisconsin. It was intriguing because the large box (about 10" high X 12" deep X 34 inches wide!) was formally a Howard Radio model from the 1920's. It was completely empty, save the metal logo plate inside the top, hinged lid. Fig. 1 shows a birds-eye view of the unaltered cabinet.

Fig. 1 Unaltered cabinet.

Someone had removed the radio chassis inside which contained the variable capacitors, transformer, tubes, batteries and all the wiring. Not only that, but the radio's large slate faceplate and all the knobs were gone as well. The faceplate had been replaced by a plain, handcrafted teak board, stained lightly to match the rest of the cabinet.

Bill suspected that the person who modified the Howard Radio cabinet had plans to either build a more modern radio inside that cabinet, or just make a nifty-looking storage box for whatever. Anyway, the price tag was just $5, so Bill snatched it up quickly, with no immediate plans for the box.

After storing that beautiful "project box" for a few weeks, Bill finally came up with a plan. Lets make it a radio again, but this time it'll be a crystal radio perhaps the world's LARGEST crystal radio.

Because Bill hadn't built anything of this magnitude before, and had almost no experience in winding large capacitance coils, he decided to contact a fellow member of our Ozaukee Radio Club, Stan Kaplan. Stan was very adept at winding a wide variety of coils and had built several crystal radios throughout the years, plus he was also a member of the Xtal Set Society. Stan welcomed the cooperative project with open arms.

It was to be a "Winter Project", but Stan wasted no time in winding the coils and filling that cavernous container with a myriad of wonderful and colorful gadgets, making it almost too pretty to close the lid! With some additional staining on the faceplate and the addition of some antique dials and knobs that Bill had been saving for something like this, the radio was ready for it's debut at our next mid-winter ham radio club meeting.

Our design for the electronics is shown in Fig. 2. Two rook-wound coils (L1 and L2) were mounted so as to be moveable with respect to each other, permitting an almost infinite range of coupling in nearly half of the huge cabinet. Nothing fancy here – two PVC pipes penetrated openings in the windings and served as guides to hand-move the coils as desired. This can be seen in Fig. 3 – the top PVC pipe is painted black and is clearly visible. Indicators made of red electrical tape circle the pipe and provide convenient logging markers for reproducing the coil settings. C_1 is mounted inside the extreme left of the cabinet. Its knob is visible on the left side of the front panel. C_2, the main tuning capacitor, is mounted near the center of the cabinet. That is the knob with the dial and pointer.

Although "purists" would use no battery driven parts in a crystal radio, we wanted to make the unit more conducive for demonstrations to large groups. Bill had a small, transistorized audio amplifier and a high quality 4-inch permanent magnet speaker in his parts box, so we agreed to add those components. The 9-volt battery that powers the amp can be seen in the back right corner of Fig. 3, with wires leading to the amp mounted near the front panel. An on/off switch and volume control can be seen on the right of the front panel, next to the panel perforations we added for the speaker.

The layout of the controls can be seen best in Fig. 4. A brass plate etched with the circuit is near the knob for C_1, the antenna tuning capacitor. Finally, the original Howard Radio Company logo is shown enlarged in Fig. 5; it is also just visible in Fig. 3 on the inside of the lid above another brass plate showing the circuit diagram.

So, does it work? You bet! With a hunk of wire for an antenna and another for a ground (connected to the metal plate screw of a wall outlet), we invariably pull in stations from local and some DX stations as well. Great fun, but surely not compact and tiny!!!

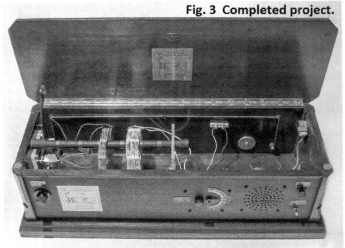

Fig. 3 Completed project.

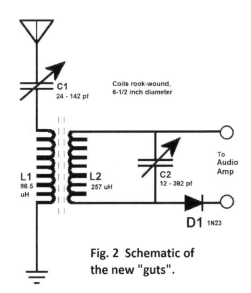

Fig. 2 Schematic of the new "guts".

Fig. 5 Original logo, still inside the lid.

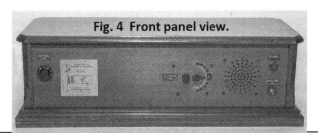

Fig. 4 Front panel view.

Bill Michna Radio

Thanks for taking interest in my cigar box radio. Sorry about missing any deadline that the society had but as I said I just received the news letter on Monday. I had just finish what you see in my photo not even knowing that you were wanting to hold a contest. so I took a shot in the dark thinking that I had nothing to lose and e mailed my picture.

I started to build this radio inside the small cedar box. I mounted a small adjustable capacitor with a knob for tuning in the front of the radio, along with 2 binding posts for antenna and ground connection. In the upper left hand corner there is a 1/4 inch phone jack plug for the high impedance ear phones. The cat whisker sits on top of the box as does the 1 1/4 inch diameter coil with about 100 turns of number 24 magnet wire. I devised an antenna to test my radio.

I built this so my grandson would have an interest in electronics. I talked him into building an oatmeal box radio for an up-coming science fair at his school.

For the record I am A Licensed ham radio operator KB9ACI and a retired sales fire protection engineer. During the past 60 years or so I have built about 30 or so crystal radios .most worked but a few did not. thanks Bill Michna

Carl Wick Radio

Please find attached a picture of my entry - two if I can get away with it (they are pretty big)! You will see the radio fits in the box I got from you - a very nice cigar box! The only modification to the box was to put some wooden posts in the corners to support the faceplate of the radio.

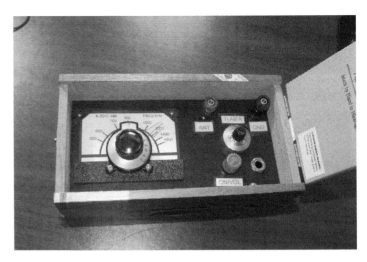

The radio itself uses a single Shottky Diode detector and contains a home-brew two transistor amplifier - situated underneath since I'm wearing hearing aids and can't hear well enough without amplification.

It has a single tuned circuit consisting of a coil wound of Litz wire on a '61 toroid. The antenna tuner consists of a home built device that inserts a ferrite rod into a loopstick coil; the coil is inside of a ferrite bead. The device will change inductance from about 70 uH to over 1 mH. It does very well tuning my vertical Ham band antenna that I used to develop the radio. The faceplate is a piece of bakelite I had and the main dial is a modification of a dial I had laying around. The only thing I'm not happy about is the use of paper labels - I tried making some decals, but could not come up with a color from my printers that you could see against the bakelite - will continue to search for a better answer. The amplifier, by the way, is a little two 2n3904 transistor AC coupled to a transistor output transformer that can easily drive headphones or a small speaker. I 'etched' a small circuit board with a Dremel tool - not enough time to make a 'real' one! I will send a much more complete description if you are interested. Had great fun making this and it works very well!

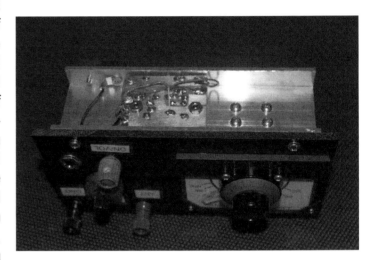

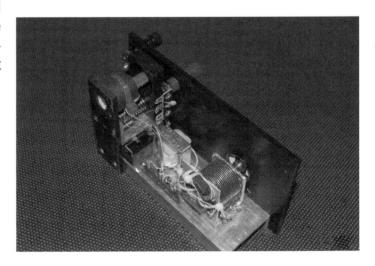

A Short Two-Way Beverage Antenna Project
By Phil Anderson, WØXI

I live in a suburban neighborhood and about two blocks from a shopping center. The city population is nearly 100,000. As such, you can imagine the reference noise level for AM and shortwave reception for each band of interest is not as quiet as a typical rural setting would be. My back yard is only 70 feet wide and 50 feet deep, thus reducing the selection of useable antennas. Furthermore, the city height limit for antennas in my neighborhood is 33 feet! My solutions so far to improve reception have been to install a 33 foot SteppIR vertical for 40 through 10 meters and a 40-meter dipole up 22 feet.

One traditional way to reduce the noise level (floor) is to install a directional antenna. These reduce the signals received from the back side, including noise, while enabling desired signals in the forward direction with some gain. Yet, towers, rotors and a Yagi antenna are costly and perhaps disturbing for the neighbors. Hence I decided to try the age old Beverage antenna, invented in 1921 by Harold Beverage. The Beverage antenna is often referred to as a traveling wave antenna. It was popular in the early days, circa 1920, and more recently on 160 meters by licensed radio amateurs.

The Beverage, like the modern Yagi, reduces signals from its back side while enhancing listening in the direction it's pointed. Results so far have been gratifying. I've made two-way CW contacts with radio amateurs in Europe and listened to US AM stations in the 8 to 10 MHz range.

Figure 1 depicts my first Beverage and supporting equipment. The antenna consists of the following: 70 feet of antenna wire strung out 8 feet above the ground from northeast to southwest (for contact with Europe from Kansas) supported by three 10 foot PVC Poles. On the northeast end, a 450 ohm terminating resistor is attached to a ground rod as noted. At the southwest end a 3-to-1 ferrite toroid UNUN step-down transformer is attached to the antenna at the top of the pole; its job is to match the 450 ohms of the traveling wave antenna to

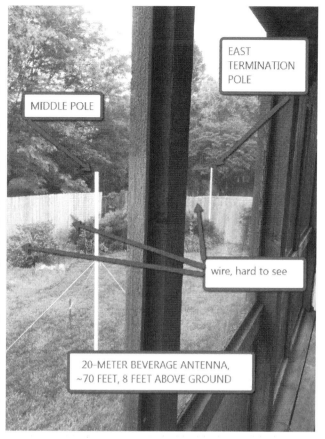

MIDDLE POLE

EAST TERMINATION POLE

wire, hard to see

20-METER BEVERAGE ANTENNA, ~70 FEET, 8 FEET ABOVE GROUND

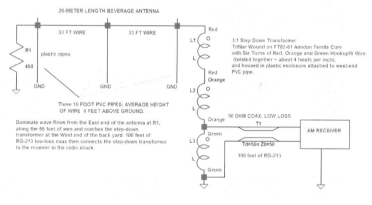

20-METER LENGTH BEVERAGE ANTENNA

33 FT WIRE   33 FT WIRE

R1   plastic pipes
450
GND   GND   GND

Three 10 FOOT PVC PIPES; AVERAGE HEIGHT OF WIRE 8 FEET ABOVE GROUND.

Dominate wave flows from the East end of the antenna at R1, along the 66 feet of wire and reaches the step-down transformer at the West end of the back yard. 100 feet of RG-213 low-loss coax then connects the step-down transformer to the receiver in the radio shack.

Red
L1
L
Red
Orange
L2
L
Orange
Green
L3
L
Green

3:1 Step Down Transformer
Trifilar Wound on FT82-61 Amidon Ferrite Core with Six Turns of Red, Orange and Green HookupW Wire (twisted together ~ about 4 twists per inch), and housed in plastic enclosure attached to west-end PVC pipe.

50 OHM COAX, LOW LOSS
T1
Td=50n Z0=50
100 feet of RG-213

AM RECEIVER

a length of 50 ohm coax going to my station. I've used this setup with my K3 Elecraft transceiver for amateur radio use, both two-way CW and AM listening. Next month I plan to try a step-up transformer into a crystal set for HF shortwave listening.

Figure 3 displays a frequency plot of an AM station received by my K3 Elecraft transmitter-receiver and P3 Panadapter at 9980 kHz via the Beverage antenna. Panadapters convert a portion of the radio spectrum received into a frequency display using an internal digital signal processor (DSP). Note that the bandwidth of the AM station shown in the figure is 10 kHz wide,

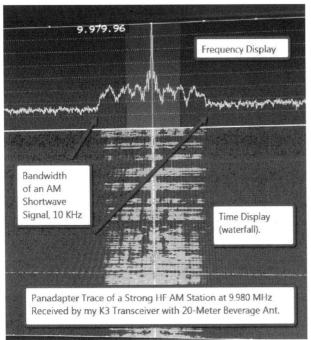

Figure 3

as expected, in the frequency display at the top. The bottom half of the figure displays the waterfall, showing the 10 kHz signal amplitude over a short period of time.

Figure 4 displays the Panadapter processed signal of WWV at 10 MHz. The carrier and sidebands represent the tones sent before the usual period of clicking that follows.

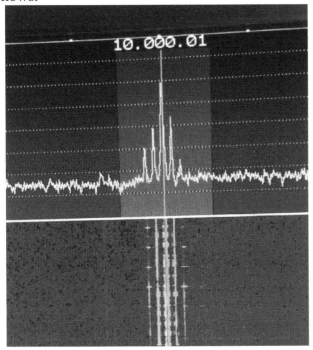

Figure 4

Results of my noise reduction efforts so far using the Beverage versus the Vertical antenna are noted in Table 1. While the results vary a bit given the time of day and from day to day, the results listed have been consistent. The only band that does not see at least an S unit and a half of background noise reduction is 15 meters. This is due, in part, to the natural reduction in cosmic and storm noise with increase in the frequency of reception. There is just less noise as one tunes the higher HF bands. The one anomaly is the fall off in improvement on 40 meters (7020 kHz). This is due in part to the length of the Beverage, only 70 feet, compared to the wavelength of the frequency in use. In addition, I designed the step-down ferrite toroid transformer for 20 meters, indicating that a few more turns or a different ferrite material for 40 meters might be helpful.

Finally, I checked the standing wave ratio (SWR) of the Beverage for the bands and specific signals listed in Table 2. Note that the SWR is below 2 to 1 for all bands except 80 and 160. This confirms that the UNUN transformer and 450 ohm resistive load match the 8 foot up/ 70 foot long Beverage well.

My first two-way HF Beverage contact was on 20 meter CW, 6/2/2015, with Gary, VE2GDI, in Quebec, Canada. He sent me a 57N signal report and I returned with a 55N. The noise level reported in my P3 Panadapter attached to the K3 (Elecraft) was 8 to 9 dBm below that obtain with my SteppIR vertical, as expected, given the directionality of the Beverage. The P3 reported noise level for the vertical was -105 dBm and for the Beverage varied between -112 and -115 dBm, nearly two S units down! My second Beverage two-way contact was with YN5SU on 17 meter CW, at 5 PM, 6/4/2015. He gave me a 55N. My output power was 10 watts into the Beverage.

What's next? My plans at this time are to rework the 450 ohm terminating resistor for 100 watt operation, and also rework the 3-to-1 ferrite transformer for 100 watts if necessary. I've been limiting CW transmission to 10 watts until I can complete that rework. I also plan to do further testing on using the Beverage as a second receive antenna in diversity reception mode.

Table 1

FREQ in (kHz)	BAND	Noise Level via P3 for Beverage (dBM)	Noise Level via P3 for Vertical (dBm)	P3 Difference Beverage minus Vertical (dBm)	Equivalent Reduction in S Units	Wavelength % of Beverage Length
21020	15	-132	-125	-7	-1.16	133
18077	17	-132	-123	-9	-1.50	117
14040	20	-119	-109	-10	-1.66	100
10120	30	-127	-111	-16	-2.66	67
7020	40	-117	-103	-14	-2.33	50

Recall that S9 is at -73 dBm, S1 is at -121 dBm and S units are spaced 6 dBm apart up to S9.

Initial attempts have been successful, transmitting on the SteppIR vertical at 100 watts and listening in my left headphone to the transmit antenna for side tone and receiving and in my right headphone to the Beverage fed via the second receiver in the Elecraft K3.

References:
Receiving Wave Antennas, Page 13-16, Chapter 13, The ARRL Antenna Book, 20th Edition, 2003-2005.
http://www.qsl.net/aa3px/beverage.htm. Google the web for the many articles about Harold Beverage and current work on Beverages by radio amateurs.
Electro-Magnetics, John Kraus, McGraw Hill, page 477. 1953. An Engineering text.
Antennas, John Kraus, McGraw Hill, pages 149, 412, 1950. An Engineering text.

Table 2

Frequency {MHz}	Band {Meters}	SWR, Measured (with Autek VA1) antenna analyzer
1.800	160	4.40
3.500	80	2.56
5.000	WWV	1.82
7.000	40	1.54
7.050	40	1.49
10.000	WWV	1.54
10.100	30	1.44
14.000	20	1.20
14.050	20	1.18
15.000	WWV	1.20
18.068	17	1.18
21.000	15	1.45

Slip Slidin' Away (With apologies to Paul Simon)

by Dan Petersen - W7OIL

In the article I wrote for the May. 2015 issue I discussed practical (perhaps unavoidable) wire antennas for the property and covenant challenged, like I am now. Gone are the days of the "RMS Titanic" antenna on hilltop acreage. Now it's "hide everything from the yard-nazis", those roving do-gooders that will nark on their best friend for the chance to feel smug. I have an antenna on the roof now that is hard to see from six feet away, much less from the ground. To put the last article in a nutshell, unless your antenna is *more* than 138 feet in length electrically it will have a capacitive reactance component. Now to make the antenna resonant at BCB frequencies you will need to add a series inductance to cancel out the reactive component. The point where the inductive and capacitive reactances are equal is called *resonance.* The easiest way to make a variable coil is to make a *slider.* The one I built is made from a 5-inch length of 4-inch PVC pipe. I was hoping for winding 88 turns of #18 enameled wire for a 630 microhenry coil but I ran out of wire at 77 turns. So I ended up with a coil of 530 microhenries. It will still work for experimental purposes.

One thing you must remember is that your results most definitely will vary. If your antenna is shorter than my 65 foot one you will need more inductance to tune it to a particular frequency. Other parameters like height above ground, proximity to metal objects, quality of ground and a few dozen other monkey-wrenches in the works will change the reactance. My 77 turn coil with #18 wire used 86 feet of wire. I would *strongly* recommend you use at least #20 wire or larger to raise the "*self-resonant*" point of your coil. And don't even THINK of using litz wire for a slider coil. Litz is a multi-strand wire with each wire insulated from the others. Start to sand litz wire for a contact area and a whole forest of hair-fine wires will fuzz up!

My slider coil has a distributed capacitance of 4.2 picofarads. The self-resonant point of this coil is

3.4 MHz, well above the frequencies of interest. The distributed capacitance cannot be *directly* measured with a meter. I used a grid-dip oscillator to determine the resonant frequency with the coil disconnected from anything, then calculated the capacitance with the known resistance, which *can* be measured with an inductance meter. Out of morbid curiosity you ask, "What happens when you go *above* the self-resonant frequency?" Well - the inductor will now "look" capacitive, and a capacitor in parallel with a capacitor does not make a very good tuned circuit!

Just Slidin' Along...

Okay, the coil is wound, how do you make the slider? You need to take a trip to your local hobby shop or hardware store for small-diameter brass square tubing. I used 1/4-inch square tubing for the slider rail and a short (1/2-inch) piece of 9/32-inch square tubing for the slider itself.

This tubing is made to slide smoothly into the next size and being square, you do not have to worry about the feeler contact rotating out of place.

The slider rail is mounted above the coil using spacers. I used 3/8-inch metal spacers. One end has a solder terminal secured to the end of the rail. the other coil contact is connected to the end of the coil winding. The other end of the winding is not connected to anything; it "floats". I used a

---

wooden knob threaded to a screw soldered to the top of the slider. From the bottom of the slider extends the feeler contact. This is made from a bit of tin-can or other thin metal that is springy. The feeler must contact an area of the coil that has had the enamel sanded away so that electrical contact will be made. In my model, with the connections on the left, the coil will *increase* in inductance. As you can see in Figure 1 the response is quite non-linear.

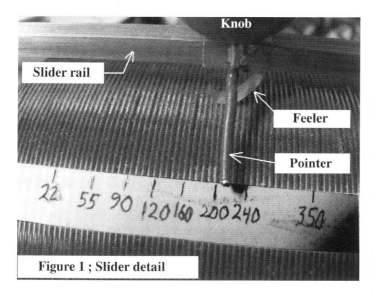

Figure 1 ; Slider detail

So Now What?

The slider won't do much good unless it is used with a receiver. Time to knock together a crystal set. In perusing the schematic in Figure 2, it comprises a plain-vanilla crystal set but with 2 differences. Figure 3 shows the differences. First; you may notice that the tuning coil is hanging a ways

off the chassis. This is to allow the tuning coil to be placed inside the slider for maximum coupling. Second; There is a six -position rotary switch mounted at the end of the coil. This is the tap switch shown in the schematic. I also installed the option of using a detector diode or a cat-whisker detector. Not much rocket science here!

Operating the Whole Shebang:

Note to the newbies - The schematic shows the slider and the tuning coil sitting next to one another. I fell for this one when I was a newbie, sometime before rocks were invented. The two coils need to be *in line* with one another.

At maximum coupling the tuning coil will be *inside* the slider coil. Changing the mutual coupling is accomplished by varying the distance between the slider coil and the tuning coil. Changing the inductance of the slider coil will tune the antenna to the desired frequency.

I built this set with a tap-switcah. The same can be done with taps sticking up from the tuning coil and connected to the detector with a wire and alligator clip. By switching between taps the selectivity and sensitivity can be varied - inversely. This means at maximum sensitivity the set is at *minimum* selectivity. Connecting the tap to "40 turns" will increase selectivity but sacrifice sensitivity. It's a juggling act.

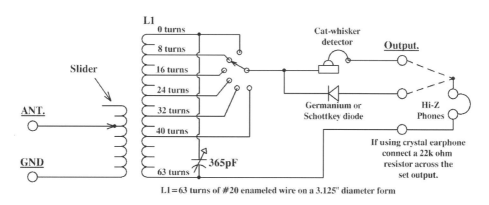

Figure 2 : The Schematic

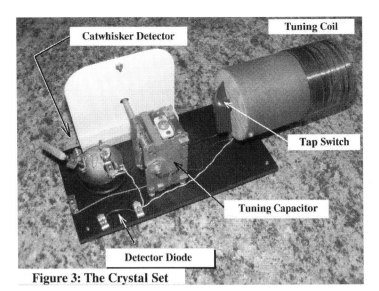

Catwhisker Detector
Tuning Coil
Tap Switch
Tuning Capacitor
Detector Diode

Figure 3: The Crystal Set

Why two different detectors? Because they *are* different. I can evaluate galenas and pyrites with the cat-whisker detector or test different diodes as detectors. I find the 1N5817 Schottkey diode works at least as well as the venerable germanium diode.

So everything is in place. The antenna and ground are connected to the slider. Headphones are connected to the output, at first using the diode. Set the tuning coil about half-inside the slider and the tap switch at maximum sensitivity (0-turns) and look for a station. If you live in a town that has more than one cop there should be a local you can pick up. Now adjust the slider for maximum volume. Setting the tap switch down towards maximum selectivity should enable you to separate stations.

By the way - placing an AM transistor radio next to the slider, tuning the radio to your favorite crock-jock, then adjusting the slider you will find the signal being boosted significantly. Just a hint for you AM-DX chasers.

I have found this combination of slider coil and crystal set to be of help here in the radio purgatory in which I now reside. Perhaps my ramblings here may help you in yours.

Keep experimenting

Amplified Crystal Cathedral
Larry Jeffers

I usually strive to build sets without batteries, but 70 year old ears make many stations come in low, even with sound-powered phones. This set won FIRST PLACE in the "homebrew" category at the Northland Antique Radio Club "Radio Daze 2015."

Another Society member, Ken Ladd won SECOND PLACE in the same category which shows that the Society is alive and well.

My cathedral set has all mahogany wood parts with a base of 5 1/4 inches wide and 10 1/2 inches deep. The front board is 12 inches wide, 141/2 inches high, and 1 1/8 inches thick. The adjustable coil coupling is made with a 1/4 inch masonry bit that has a ball bearing follower giving movement of one inch to four turns of the crank.

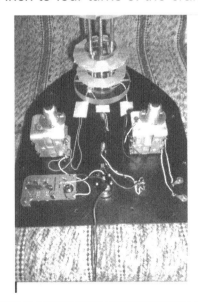

There are also some hand made parts in the coupler assembly. The cat whisker detector, binding posts and hubs to mount the dials were machined from brass. The brackets on the rear of the tuning capacitors were machined from aluminum. The dust covers are four inch PVC pipe with pipe caps. Any magnetic phones will work well from telephone receivers on up to good old vintage phones of any kind. Was this project fun? YES! Is it overkill?....Maybe.

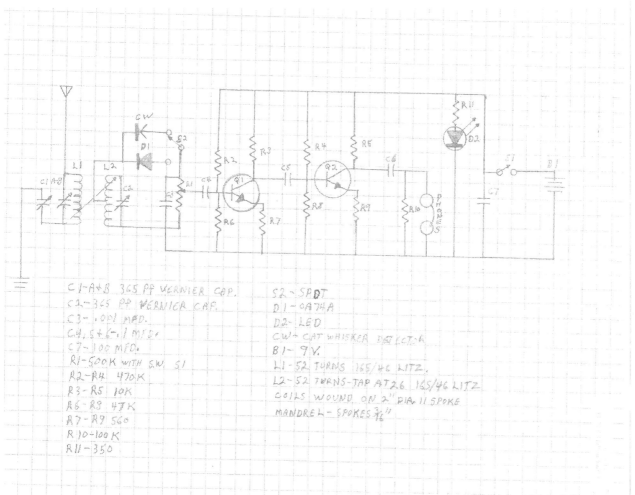

C1-A+B 365 Pf VERNIER CAP.
C2-365 Pf VERNIER CAP.
C3-.001 MFD.
C4,5+6-.1 MFD.
C7-100 MFD.
R1-500K WITH SW. S1
R2-R4 470K
R3-R5 10K
R6-R8 47K
R7-R9 560
R10-100K
R11-350

S2~SPDT
D1-0A74A
D2-LED
CW~CAT WHISKER DETECTOR
B1~ 9V.
L1-52 TURNS 165/46 LITZ.
L2-52 TURNS-TAP AT 26 165/46 LITZ
COILS WOUND ON 2" DIA. 11 SPOKE
MANDREL - SPOKES 3/16"

MK484 in a Cigar Box
Lewis Ball

I took your challenge to modify a MK 484 a.m. radio mini kit. The challenge was do I modify the cigar box or change the layout of the kit. The box was too nice to change leaving only one choice. I made the following changes some of the decals I photocopied and enlarged so that I could use them near the air variable capacitor. I cut a 1/8 inch black plastic sheet to fit inside the box. I also cut one quarter inch clear plastic to fit on top of the black plastic.

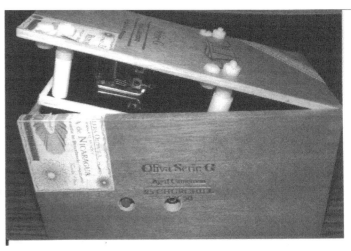

I placed the front panel copy between the two sheets of plastic below that the capacitor in place and mounted it on the lid. I also had one 1/8 black plastic sheet cut to the same size as the box and placed it on rails near the bottom of the cigar box. To that I mounted the ferrite rod antenna on the hinge end of the box.

To the circuit board I made modifications using 4 - 40 x 3/8" bolts placing them in the 10 solder points. I placed 4-40 nuts on the bolts of the board, the bottom. one being tight the upper one being left lose so I can use a spade lug so I can change capacitors or antennas just by taking the original ones out and replacing the new components.

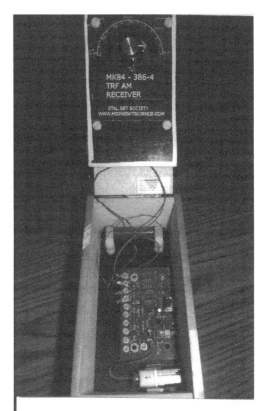

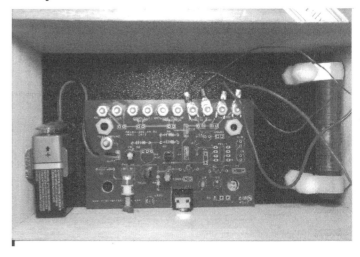

Robert "Bob" Ryan, Jr.
A Short Story of Meeting A Radio Designer and Builder
By Randall Shreve KD7PCW

Back in the 1990s I was with Northrop Aircraft and one of our plants was located in Anaheim, California. Right down the street from this plant was a very nice electronics store. This, my friends, was the real deal, a true electronics store and was not one of the "Rat Shack" chain stores that seemed to Dot the landscape.

During my lunch breaks I would often visit this electronics store. In one of the glass display cases were these beautifully handcrafted radio sets. At a single glance from afar one might think that it was a display case of radio memorabilia.

However, these radios were not antiques, but were newly made handcrafted crystal and very unique "super regenerative" tube radios. Each radio was labeled "Handcrafted in America by Bob Ryan."

My personal interests in crystal sets stemmed from my grandfather's stories of growing up in upper New York State listening to local broadcasts on his cat's whisker radio set. Unintentionally my grandfather turned me into a radio addict when he presented me with an Olsen crystal radio set at the tender age of ten years old. The magic of the crystal set was powerful juju. Later in my "long hair" days I worked in the Broadcast Industry for a few local radio stations and often a crystal set would come in handy when listening to transmitter output.

By the time I was first introduced to these wonderfully handcrafted "Ryan" receivers in the 1990s I was a "radio junkie" deep into SWLing. Married and with children meant monetary priorities went elsewhere as these Ryan custom sets fetched a price beyond my normal means to justification to the XYL. So being the good little radio junkie I saved up my lunch money with the hopes that by the time I had enough funding squirreled away one of these sets would still be available as these babies seemed to fly off the shelve.

Regenerative radios… These were interesting and exotic rigs that fascinated me. I soon found that there is nothing that compares to the thrill of passing over a station's heterodyne whistle while tuning one of these sets only to come back and fine tune and adjust to obtain perfect audio. Honest, I really tried hard not to drool on the glass counter while test-driving these Ryan radios. My lunchtime visitations became so regular that to save time the proprietor got to the point of just pulling the radios out of the cabinet prior to my noontime visits.

As I mentioned, these sets were by no means inexpensive, but the level of detail, the beautiful craftsmanship, perfectly wound coils, custom printed handbooks made these radios something really special. Finely the day came and I purchased a Ryan regenerative set. It was a tough choice as the Bob Ryan crystal set (called the "Red Robin") that I had also been playing with was a real treat. I had never seen or listened to a set that performed like the "Red Robin " it was truly an amazing set and even with just a short six foot piece of scrap wire and no ground this crystal set really pulled in the local stations with exceptional selectivity. It was the cat's pajamas of crystal sets!

The Ryan regenerative set was just too fun so I decided on this unique multi-band one tube receiver. Now that I owned one of these handcrafted radios I wanted to meet this Ryan fellow. He was somewhere in Anaheim, how hard could it be, right?

All I could get out of the owner of the electronics store was that Bob Ryan was a local guy who builds radios as a hobby. "Yeah, well Bob kind of comes and goes, we see him when he needs some tubes" was it. Bob Ryan was not listed in the phone book and the Internet was no help. So Bob Ryan was a mystery man. As the decades rolled past I would, from time-to-time, run up his name on the Internet with no success. Occasionally I would see a "Bob Ryan" mentioned in a Popular Communications magazine article. Again, I would fail to local Mr. Ryan as he was simply "off the grid."

Sometime after joining the XTAL Set Society I came across a short article in the Society's Newsletter written by Bob Ryan. My conclusion was it had to be the same fellow and with the help of "Queen Mum" after 20+ years I was finally able to introduce myself to this elusive radio builder.

From our first contact Bob Ryan proved to be a true gentleman, extremely friendly and knowledgeable radio builder.

A fascinating self taught radio engineer and set builder, Bob picked up the love for creating radios during his boyhood years as World War II gripped the nation. Bob, an avid reader, studied designs by reading old "Short Wave Craft" magazines and collecting discarded radios for parts. Bob shared graphic stories of the hazards that young radio builders going through old sets had to be mindful of as new radio parts were hard to obtain due to the War Effort: *"Ahhhh, spiders, geez!"* were Bob's words.

With salvaged parts and various designs at hand the young Ryan built crystal and regenerative radios that enabled him and others to listen to the world at war. These childhood radio intercepts were the stuff that, are now reenacted in movies today, gives chills when I think of how it must have been, late at night with his "cans" tightly pressed upon his ears, young Bob followed the war as it raged in Europe, Africa and the Pacific. Imagine what it must have been like to hear war news, enemy propaganda and music as the RF came dancing down Bob's antenna.

Once the war was over his love of building radios and studying various crystal and Armstrong based designs did not go to the wayside. Instead, Bob continued to read articles and correspond with many noted designers and authors of the day building and testing receivers as time permitted.

During his teenage years Bob spent time in Japan studying the culture that had just a few short years before been our enemy. As a side note, during 1956 Bob was in close proximity with the famous Japanese aviator that had shot down the equally famous U.S. Marine Ace "Papa" Boyington as well as meeting several retired Japanese Naval Admirals (Bob related that these Admirals were some of the most charming people that he had ever met in his travels).

Sometime during the early 1950s Bob's parents moved into a nice home in Anaheim, California while building a chain of Women's Clothing Stores in the Southern California area. Bob continued to experiment with various designs as he purchased war surplus test equipment and other gear mainly for the vast selection of quality parts. Bob commented more than once that many of these designs sounded better on paper then in actual performance.

What Bob and I later found to be ironic was that his parent's first store, in which he worked, was located in the Lakewood City Mall. My Mother, with me in reluctant tow, shopped at the Ryan's store. What a hoot for Bob and I to discover that we had both shared the same sidewalk as well as been visitors of the then very popular Clifton's Cafeteria located at the Mall. Wow, talk about small world!

By this point Bob was now living in Hemet, California after moving out of the city of Anaheim. During his time in Anaheim he watched it grow from orange groves, to Disneyland to a major metro-area of Los Angeles.

Gosh, we both wished that we had somehow meet up decades earlier. However, a deep friendship quickly developed centered upon our common interests. Bob's ability to consume books truly amazed. Same with the use of his favorite writing instrument, the typewriter.

No Internet for Bob, happily calling himself a dinosaur as the Internet would just take time away from helping care for his aging friends in the retirement community of Hemet. Ah, the typewriter… In short order Bob got me hooked on something that many of us in today's world of the Internet Superhighway have forgotten, the simple joy of receiving a real letter in the Postbox. Truly, try it sometime and you will rediscover Bob Ryan's little secret, the posted letter means more to the soul than Internet e-mails!

Interestingly Bob's first purchased "kit" receiver was one of Elmer Osterhoudt's popular Modern Radio Labs 3Q5 tube regenerative rigs with plug in coils. As a young man Bob became friends with Mr. & Mrs. Osterhoudt and spent many Sundays together back in the day. Bob was also acquainted with Hugo Gernsback, famous for the "Shortwave Craft" and "Radio Craft" magazines of the 1930s, 40's.

By the time I met Bob he had given up bench work due to health reasons. However, as my personal passion for regenerative receivers grew Bob shared concepts, technical information, tube types and how he manufactured the various sheet metal and other components.

My 1990 purchase of the Ryan regenerative receiver earlier mentioned was Bob's melding of concepts around a main design platform "The Worcester's 1933 Oscillodyne." This receiver uses a single #30 tube with 1.5 volts for the "A" battery and 45 volts for the "B" battery with various plug in coils for both AM broadcast and various popular shortwave bands. With a good ground and short random wire antenna this regenerative receiver really performs. It's a bit of a tiger to first learn how to control regeneration, but once learned it's a sweetheart.

Some readers might find it of interest that in the fact there are countless thousands, if not millions, of regenerative receivers are still in daily use from controlling Industrial devices to home garage door openers. The 101-year-old design is still alive and well! Over the course of years I have found that, at times (in fact often) that a well made regenerative receiver will out perform many modern shortwave sets in its ability to dig out weak signals.

In the year 2000 Bob had taken another older design, the "Short Wave Craft" magazine award winning "1932 Harold Johnson Circuit" and performed a similar melding of design modifications for a another one tube regenerative receiver. By this point Bob had built and tested hundreds of different designs both foreign and domestic and felt that for the minimal part count required that this design was a true winner. One of the several interesting design changes that Bob introduced into this 1932 creation was the use of a three-foot whip antenna. Due to antenna restrictions at Bob's retirement QTH, Bob recognized that antenna restrictions were going to be a real problem for many of us now, and in the future. Experimentation with shorter than normal antennas became a focus out of necessity. Indeed, with a good set of headphones this little receiver with its 3-foot whip is a surprising performer.

From tubes to antennas, to inventors, from science to the greater world at large Bob Ryan's motto "History is my religion and Shortwave Radio is my Magic Carpet" along with his up-beat persona "I laugh at old insomnia and just hop to my shortwave receiver in my living room if I cannot sleep" and his desire to help his neighbors shows optimism with kindness. Truly, the high road approach to life.

Last year when I indicated that I was going to run an amateur radio event station on 20 meters in celebration for the 100th year anniversary of the first transcontinental telephone line, Bob quickly sent me a book that contained an original in-depth article about the transcontinental telephone line. The article even included interviews with Alexander Graham Bell, type of copper wire used in the construction as well as how many telephone poles were required for this historical and now forgotten event. Amazing!

Thanks to the Xtal Set Society and "Queen Mum" I am a lucky fellow to follow my quest to meet up with this amazing builder and could write volumes about my friend Bob Ryan, so much so that I wouldn't know where to exactly stop, except to say that on May 5th of this year Bob Ryan went Silent Key.

It was my honor and privilege to have been Bob Ryan's last "Radio Scout" and while he will be deeply missed, he was a radioman who left his positive mark on those he touched. He truly loved the Xtal Set Society and it's wonderful newsletter as a meeting place for likeminded radio enthusiasts to write and share ideas. Bob was a humble man and once told me "*its not so much that I love shortwave, yes I can and will sit still and listen to cultural music even in a foreign language, but its the simple fact that each time I flip the switch I am still amazed that I am listening on a radio that I made with my own hands.*"

I don't think that it gets any better then that... 73

inspired by 1932 Australian MYSTERY
CRYSTAL SET by "Proton" of Brisbane
Bob Ryan of California - 2012

Editor's note: One of Bob's beginner radios is featured in the September 2012 issue. I have repeated the picture here.

Chip Ohleiser's MK484

I built this mk484 chip radio using many XTAL SET SOCIETY parts. It was built about 2 years ago.

It works great, and is sensitive and loud.

FEATURES

MK484 single chip radio chip from Xtal set society
LM386 audio amplifier for plenty loud audio
Large 2 pound magnet oval speaker for full range audio and loud sound
Loopstick antenna internal to set
Vernier slow-tuning tuning capacitor from XTAL SET SOCIETY
Internal 9V battery, about 60 days life
Plastic high impact case
SENSITIVE! 70 DB dynamic range with agc contained in the mk484 chip

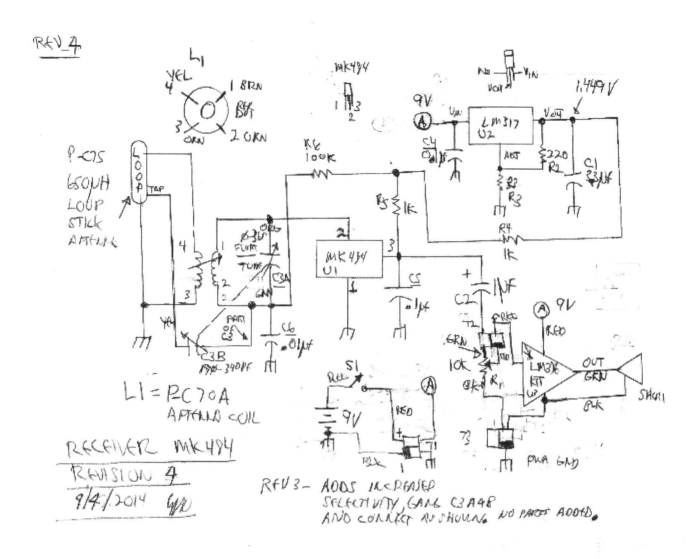

REV 4

P-C75
650µH
LOOP
STICK
ANTENNA

L1 = P-C70A
ANTENNA COIL

RECEIVER MK484
REVISION 4
9/4/2014

REV3 - ADDS INCREASED
SELECTIVITY, GAIN C3A4B
AND CORRECT AS SHOWN NO PARTS ADDED.

MK484 BCB RECEIVER	DESCRIPTION	P/N	QTY	REF DES	
	8 OHM SPEAKER 4X4 8 OHMS S300SA	70115843	1	SPKR 1	$4.00
	AMP AUDIO LM386 KITS AND PARTS DOT CPM	LM386	1	LM386	$8.00
	BATTERY 9 VOLT BATTERY 4 PACK	23-866	1	B1	$2.75
	capacitor, .01µF, 50V	55047551	1	C6	$0.47
	capacitor, .1 µF, 50V	55047557	2	C4, C5	$0.47
	capacitor, 0-365 PF MAIN	365 AIR VARIABLE	1	C3	$10.95
	capacitor, 1.0 µF, 25V	55047773	1	C2	$0.47
	capacitor, 3.3 µF, 25V	55047829	1	C1	$0.47
	CASE PLASTIC CASE	-	1	CASE	$7.00
	COIL ANTENNA COIL	P-C70-A	1	L1	$8.95
	COIL ANTENNA LOOP STICK 650 UH	P-C75	1	ANTENNA	$2.95
	HARDWARE, MISC	-	-		$2.00
	IC LM317 REGULATOR CHIP TO-220 PKG	LM317 TO220	1	U2	$1.50
	IC MK484 RADIO IC	MK484	1	U1	$1.50
	KNOB BLUE	274-0403	2	KB	$2.99
	PWB, PROTYPING, BARE	276-0148	1	PWB	$2.49
	RESISTOR 5 K OHM VAR AUDIO TAPER	271-1720	1	R1	$3.49
	resistor, 1 K	271-1118	2	R4, R5	$0.30
	resistor, 100K	271-1347	1	R6	$0.30
	resistor, 33 OHM	271-1104	1	R3	$0.30
	resistor, 220 OHM	271-1313	1	R2	$0.30
	SWITCH SPST		1	S1	$3.00

NOTES:
REV 3 NO PARTS ADDED
COST REDUCED RESISTORS 5 PACK, ONLY NEED 1
COST REDUCED BATTERY 4 PACK, ONLY NEED 1

TOTAL COST $51.48

Impedances of Crystal Sets
By Phil Anderson, WØXI

{Editor's Note: We received an email note from Ron, K5RGM, on the Beverage Antenna article by Phil in the July 2015 issue. "I read the article by Phil on his Beverage antenna. On page two, last line first paragraph, Phil states 'Next month I plan to try a step-up transformer from the Beverage into a crystal set for HF shortwave listening.' This indicates to me that the impedance for a crystal set is well above 450 Ω. In all the web sites that I have been to, I have not found impedance stated for crystal radios. Is this because the impedances vary widely from set to set? Is there a "ball park" impedance for crystal radios?"]

All homebrew crystal sets will vary from one another in a number of ways: the type and characteristics of their attached antenna, connection to a varied ground, arrangement of the coil or coils in the set – including the Q and those coils, the type of detector used, the type of audio step-down transformer used for matching phones – if used, the type of phones or crystal ear piece used, and more. As a result, one cannot really define a specific impedance for crystal sets. At the same time, *some long-time crystal radio enthusiasts have loosely grouped crystal sets by the effective impedance of the diode detector used.* As was discovered in the last few decades, a high-impedance diode can assist a crystal set utilizing a high-impedance antenna and tank circuit (hi Q), thus improving selectivity and weak signal detection. In addition, a matching transformer must be added to match the lower impedance of the headphones. The result is a high-Q set wherein the impedances before and after the detector diode match its crossover resistance (1).

To get a feel for the operation of such a set and to estimate the best values for the components given a specific diode, we'll examine the circuits shown in Figures 1A, 1B and 1C. Let's start with 1A, which is a schematic of a simple single-tank (LC) crystal set. The antenna is shown series-coupled with a variable tuning cap (C3) and attached to the parallel tuned circuit (C2 and L1). Since nearly all crystal sets are made for the AM broadcast band, the length of a single wire antenna will be much less than a quarter-wavelength from 550 to 1500 kHz. As such the antenna circuit can be modeled as a generator in series with its effective resistance and capacitance. This antenna is then connected in series with a variable antenna tuning cap (C3) which is adjusted to minimize the total antenna capacitance to a desired value. A desired side effect of this action is that the antenna resistance is increased.

We then transform the antenna circuit of Figure 1A into the antenna circuit shown in Figure 1B as a voltage source with R2 and C4. R2 represents the transformed antenna resistance and C4 is the transformed capacitance. It turns out that R2 will have a large value, roughly in the 80k to 500k range. C4 will vary but is generally small and near in value to C2 in Figure 1A. C4 can then be added in parallel with the tank variable capacitor C2, resulting in a single cap in parallel with coil L1.

Looking on the audio side of Figure 1B, we see the audio load, R1. Generally this will consist of a step-up transformer, RF bypass capacitor and headphones. The whole audio circuit transformed to the primary (high side) of the transformer represents the audio load on the detector diode. For optimum performance, this load is matched to the diode's crossover resistance. (See Ben Tongue's website reference for details on determining the detector diode crossover resistance.)

Finally, let's resonate L1, C2 and C4 in Figure 1B and combine that with V1 and R2 (the antenna circuit). The result is a voltage source with source resistance R3 in Figure 1C. R3 and the effective audio circuit resistance R1 are designed to be close in value to the diode resistance for maximum signal reception.

This circuit might seem a bit odd. One usually expects when a generator is matched to a load that there are only two impedances, that of the generator and the load. For that basic circuit, we know that maximum power is transferred from a generator to the load when the generator and load resistances are equal. Surprisingly, with our high-resistance diode crystal set, we've ended up with three resistors in series for the model, as noted in Figure 1C: the antenna and tuned circuit equivalent resistance (as a generator impedance), the diode resistance and the equivalent audio resistance (as a load). A second surprise is that this combination, while not optimal, comes very close to transferring maximum power when all three resistances are about the same.

Just curious, I ran out a series of calculations shown in Table 1 below using 1 ohm resistors as nominal to keep the math simple. Note that when all three resistances are close to each other, e.g. 1, 1, and 1, the power delivered is nearly optimal. With the diode resistance kept at 1, I then increased the generator and load resistances with various values, noting that the power delivered was less than that at 1-1-1 or 1-1-2. The only combinations exceeding this were those listed in the first set of numbers at the top of the table. In all cases the source voltage was held constant.

The circuit transformations from Figure 1A through Figure 1C may be carried out using a number of circuit analysis techniques: equating a current source to a voltage source and vice versa, resonating a tuned circuit so as to represent its impedance as a resistance and substituting an R and C in series for a different R and C in parallel at a specific frequency. These techniques are described in circuit analysis textbooks.

References:
1. B. Tongue, http://www.bentongue.com At this site, Ben lays out the details of the impedance of diodes when used in a high-Z crystal set. This site also describes in detail the concept of diode crossover resistance. This is roughly the resistance of the diode midway between the point wherein the diode begins to conduct and the typical break point (like 0.6 volts for a silicon diode).
2. Ed Richley, "The Design of Unpowered AM Receivers Using Detectors Made From Rocks," The Xtal Set Society Newsletter, Vol 5, No 2, March 1, 1995, available at www.midnight.science.com.
3. https://en.wikipedia.org/wiki/Saturation_current
4. Phil Anderson, WØXI, "A Great Teacher: The Crystal Set," QEX Magazine (ARRL), Sept-Oct, 2008

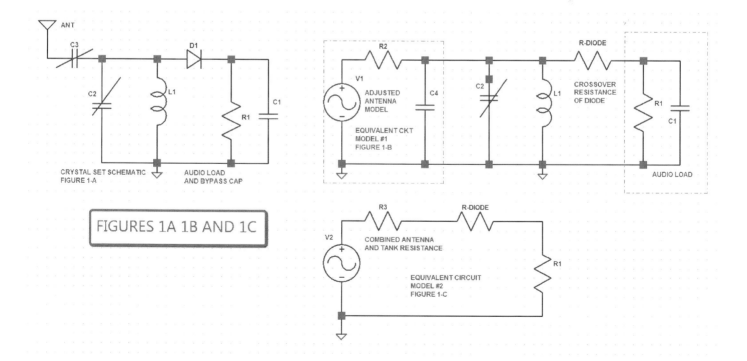

FIGURES 1A 1B AND 1C

| THREE RESISTOR MATCH PHIL, WØXI | | 8/6/2015 | | |
rms Voltage Source	R1 Rant generator	R2 fixed Rdiode diode	R3 Raudio load	power at load
1	0.6	1	1	0.148
1	0.7	1	1	0.137
1	0.8	1	1	0.128
1	0.9	1	1	0.119
1	1	1	0.6	0.089
1	1	1	0.7	0.096
1	1	1	0.8	0.102
1	1	1	0.9	0.107
1	1	1	1	0.111
1	1	1	2	0.125
1	1	1	3	0.120
1	1	1	4	0.111
1	1	1	5	0.102
1	1	1	6	0.094
1	2	1	1	0.063
1	2	1	2	0.080
1	2	1	3	0.083
1	2	1	4	0.082
1	2	1	5	0.078
1	2	1	6	0.074
1	3	1	1	0.040
1	3	1	2	0.056
1	3	1	3	0.061
1	3	1	4	0.063
1	4	1	5	0.050
1	4	1	6	0.050
1	4	1	1	0.028
1	4	1	2	0.041
1	4	1	3	0.047
1	4	1	4	0.049
1	4	1	5	0.050
1	4	1	6	0.050

Power out for 3 resistors in series, rather than just two for maximum power transfer to load.

a coating of carpenter's glue, I glued a basswood strip to the inside of the tube. Brass-plated steel eye-screws were then mounted through the tube's cardboard and secured into the basswood strip on the inside of the tube. Small pieces of basswood attached to the inside of the tube can act as a coil mounting to a breadboard. If you were to use a plastic bottle, removing the label and leaving the sticky label mounting adhesive gives you a surface that grips the wire bette that you are using to make a coil.

Some ideas from Ron Sindric

Salutations My Crystal Queen !

Not much to say. I've been playing around in isolation with some things for crystal radio building. Some of what I am sending you might already be in the lexicon of crystal set building. Some of my ideas will hopefully be unique and useful.

For making electrical capacitors, there is adhesively backed aluminum available in hardware stores. This stuff will conduct and is used to seal HVAC ducts, rain gutters, etc. I got mine at a MENARD'S STORE.

After fiddling around making twists while winding multi-tap coils, I decided to do things a bit different. Starting with a cardboard tube reinforced with

To provide a cheap ground plane for my radios, I cut up some large beverage cans and attached the aluminum from the can to the bottom of the breadboard with aluminum tacks. Drilling through the aluminum, a ground **FAHNSTOCK CLIP** is mounted to the top-side of the radio breadboard. The aluminum base is then covered with some closed cell foam cut from a yoga matt. If a person does not have beverage cans around, they can pick up disposable turkey roasting pans or even thick aluminum foil typically found in the kitchen section of your local discount stores.

EURO-STYLE terminal strip connectors can be used surface mounted on a wooden breadboard breadboard to provide an easy way to quickly re-wire a radio circuit. Finding **FAHNSTOCK CLIPS** is becoming more and more difficult every day. So, I've started using either brass or brass-plated steel "angle brackets" along with machine screws and thumb-screw nuts for antenna and ground connections.

The same **EU TERMINAL STRIPS** can be used in place of **FAHNSTOCK CLIPS** for attaching the pin-plug ends from old-style headphones to a breadboarded radio.

If you have a cardboard coil form that is not the right diameter, the tube can be carefully cut down its length. A strip of curved cardboard from another paper tube can be carpenter's glued to the inside edge of the tube along the cut. This would allow for an expansion of the tube to make a larger diameter coil. Cutting a strip from one edge along the original slit and using the glued-in strip would allow the builder to create a slightly smaller diameter coil mounting tube.

Small pieces of basswood mounted to the inside bottom of a coil form would allow the builder to easily mount her or his coils vertically to a wooden breadboard.

I am attaching a few pix for reference. If even one person takes to just one of these ideas, then I will be a happier man.

A modern Eddystone AW2 saga
by Dan Petersen - W7OIL

In the mid 1930's a radio receiver was introduced in Great Britain called the "Eddystone All-World Two". The radio was targeted to amateur radio operators and was a simple, inexpensive way to receive both amateur and commercial transmissions. The cost of £3.17.6 (three pounds, 17 shillings, 6 pence) was a good weeks wage for many folks.

When WW broke out in September, 1939 a large number of British hams had one of these receivers. When WW2 started the order came down from the government for all amateur transmitting equipment to be locked away - literally. There was a need for qualified morse code listeners (all hams were then) to monitor radio traffic and report their findings to the government. These intrepid patriots were known as Volunteer Interceptors. A huge amount of enemy signals were copied, then forwarded to the Bletchly Park's cipher-wizards to decipher. The Eddystone All-World Two was a major player in this endeavor.

So I want to build a replica? It would be practically impossible to make an exact copy as (#1) It was a British radio with British parts, some custom made by or for Eddystone and (#2) the expense for such a project would bust my bank. My toy-money fund is pretty small. So how about a "working replica" for want of a better term? This I may be able to handle with help from "OIL's Junquebox". The project now becomes "Eddystone 2015".

Engaging in a "spider hunt" through the dusty recesses of the "junquebox" I find a steel cabinet that is almost the same dimensions of the original. It was full of unsorted parts so some sorting was in order to empty it out. Too bad that it does not have a hinged lid on top as does the original but I can work around that.

Nineteen-thirties Mullard vacuum tubes are not exactly big-box store items here in the "Colonies" nor is the dual 1-microfarad Custom Eddystone

capacitor used in this rig. One thing that can be "fudged" is the special *detented* bandset capacitor. Bandset? Think of it as "coarse tuning". This enabled the bandset capacitor to be "selected" to ten discrete positions in the original. Solution? I took the detent assembly from an old rotary switch and mated it with a 150 picofarad variable capacitor (see Figure 1). Alas, my "copy" has only seven settings rather than the original ten. Ya' can't have everything!

Figure 1

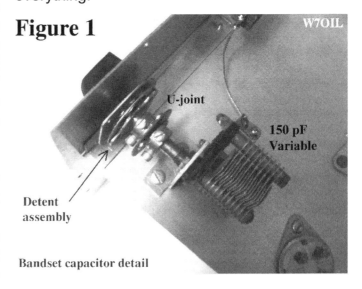

Bandset capacitor detail

The original circuit had an unusual design feature that had the filament battery's negative terminal connected through a 1000-ohm resistor to ground. The audio section's grid resistor *was* connected to ground thus imparting a negative potential to the grid of the Mullard tube. With my desire to use the original circuit as much as possible, substituting American tubes for the British ones. So construction began.

I do not think I need to go into all of the sordid details about the construction but I will touch on the chassis. This I made from pieces of sheet aluminum fastened together with 1/2" by 1/2" aluminum angle available from home improvement stores. This angle is 1/16" thick and is ideal for all sorts of projects.

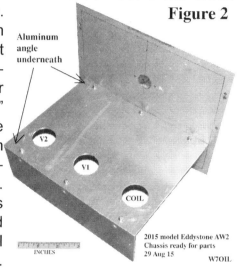

Figure 2

Aluminum angle underneath

V2

V1

COIL

2015 model Eddystone AW2
Chassis ready for parts
29 Aug 15

INCHES

W7OIL

The three 1.25" holes I cut out on my drill-press using a "cone-bit" available at Harbor Freight. Wear gloves when drilling stuff like this. If the drill catches you could be in for a visit to the emergency room to bandage where your fingers used to be. You don't want "Stumpy" as a nickname anyway.

All the chassis plates are secured with 4-40 screws with clearance holes in the plates and tapped holes in the aluminum-angle pieces. Back in the March, 2008 *Newsletter* I wrote an article called "The Classy Chassis". That chassis used lexan plastic plates but the idea is the same.

The schematic for the Eddystone 2015 is almost pure "Yank". Since I am using American tubes the need to include circuitry for a "C" bias is not necessary. I have a hunch that the British "valves" needed a negative bias on the control grid to work properly. One thing I *have* adopted from the "Royalists" is picking the audio from the plate of the detector rather than on the "other side" of the feedback winding. This makes routing the audio to the AF amplifier much easier since you do not have to route the audio from the coil all the way back past the detector plate to the AF tube.

I have a confession to make:

I *did* wire the circuit using the English schematic, rather than the "American" one shown. When I first fired the Eddystone 2015 up no smoke was released from anywhere. That's good news. The bad news was that it crackled, popped and made generally unhealthy sounding noises in the headphones. I pulled all the rabbits out of my hat trying to make it at least resemble a working radio but alas, my wizard's wand failed me. So, get away from this thing and go assuage my disappointment with eating dinner - something tasty, deep-fried and no nutritional qualities. The next day I had a simple plan. Tear it down to parade rest and start over. Hence the "American" schematic in Figure 3.

Figure 4 shows the layout topside. The bandspread (fine tuning) capacitor is mounted on a right-angle bracket with a universal shaft coupler between it and the tuning drive. At least this part of the set looks pretty much like the original. The underside (Figure 5)is quite different but the parts density is about the same.

The Finishing Touches:
The tuning dial and the two "dial-plates" for the bandset and regeneration were done using AutoCad and my printer. Similar success could be had with CorelDraw or similar programs. I painted the front panel and the cabinet with "Leather Brown" spray paint.

Fire it up...again:
Smoke test time again. Hook up the batteries and...nothing. I try my best incantations, none of them repeatable in polite society, and gird myself for battle. I found one unsoldered joint. Ah, we have noise in the headphones. Advance the regeneration and...nothing. When that happens with a "jenny" (slang for a regenerative receiver) swap the two feedback wires. Shazam! We have regeneration! I lightly tap the top of the detector

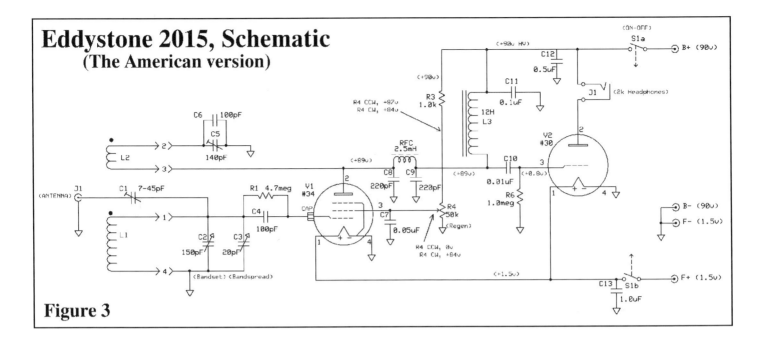

Eddystone 2015, Schematic
(The American version)

Figure 3

tube and hear a healthy "bonging" due to micro-phonics. Get used to it - most jennys do this. Now for the acid test...

I have find this set to be a good performer on the 40 meter ham band and on the 49 meter SWBC band. The tuning is smooth as is the regeneration control. It acts just like a 1935 radio should - a bit drifty, no AGC and usually several signals being heard at the same time when the band is busy. But you get to hear signals the way the British VI's and hams of the period did.

I am amazed to think that this is the **70th** article I have written for the XSS *Newsletter*. I wish to thank the Queen Mum, Her Prince Consort and best of all, my readers in sticking with me. Dan Petersen - W7OIL

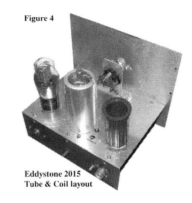

Figure 4

**Eddystone 2015
Tube & Coil layout**

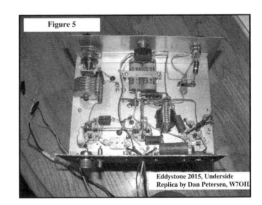

Figure 5

**Eddystone 2015, Underside
Replica by Dan Petersen, W7OIL**

Three Detectors: Diode, JFET and STOCK OPTIONS

By Phil, WØXI

Detector: a device or instrument designed to detect the presence of a particular object or substance and to emit a signal in response.

That definition is quite broad; yet, we can see that it applies to the crystal set detector. The particular object we are referring to here is radio waves in the lower high frequency bands. A crystal radio detector (D1), like that in Figure 1, samples the AM radio signal – our object – and strips off the audio of that wave.

Figure 1 depicts a simple AM crystal radio. L2 couples the energy collected by the antenna and transfers it to the tuned circuit, L1 – C1. The signal is then rectified by the diode, D1, and is transferred to the load, R1. C2 is added to strip off any remaining radio frequency energy, leaving the audio signal which is dissipated in R1. R1 can take many forms; but is usually the combination of a step-down audio transformer followed by a pair of earphones – at least the simple sets in the early days of radio.

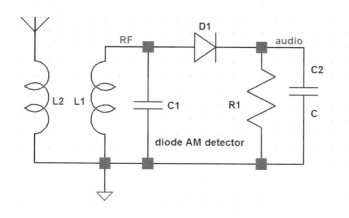

Figure 1

When a single-ended detector, like that in Figure1 is used, the detector curve required to emit the audio at its output is that shown in Figure 2, a typical diode curve. When the RF signal is positive relative to the voltage across the load, R1, the diode will conduct, thus reestablishing the voltage across R1. When the RF signal swings below the voltage at R1 it does not conduct any

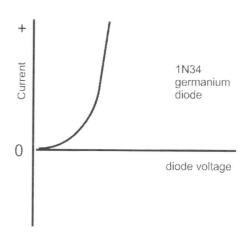

Figure 2

current. Over time, the output into the headphones is a rough duplicate of the audio placed on the radio carrier back at the radio station.

Some draw diode curves like that shown in Figure 4, with a horizontal line at essentially zero voltages followed by a straight diagonal line – nearly straight upward. In general, the curves for diodes vary by part number and makeup. In general the diode is considered a square-law device.

Figure 3 presents an AM receiver that makes use of a Junction Field Effect Transistor, or JFET as the detector. The characteristic curves of JFETs are similar to the old triode and pentode tubes of the early days of powered radios.

C6-L2-C7 make up an antenna tuner. The signal generated by the tuner is then magnetically coupled into the traditional crystal radio tank circuit, L1-C3. The signal is then AC-coupled onto the gate of the JFET. And here is where this radio departs from the traditional crystal set as in Figure 1, the input impedance of the JFET at the gate is very high. As such little or no current is drawn by the JFET. It simply samples the voltage which reappears at the source of the JFET, that is, at the top of R2. This arrangement thus preserves the voltage generated at the top of the RX TANK, L1-C3. Due to this arrangement the amplitude of the radio signal is preserved; that is, the detector does not drawn down the energy of the thank, as happens with the set in Figure 1. Thus stronger signals are maintained; more stations can be heard. The output for the set is taken from the source, i.e. the voltage atop R2. The audio portion of the circuit can thus be the same as that used in Figure 1.

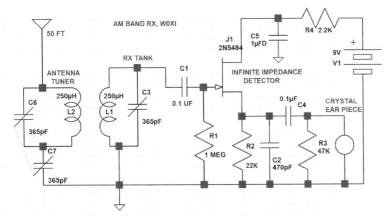

Figure 3

Finally, we arrive at the stock option detector. Why do I call it that and how do stocks or options on stocks have anything to do with detectors in crystal sets? That's a fair question!

Let's return to our original definition of a detector: a device or instrument designed to detect the presence of a particular object or substance and to emit a signal in response. Well guess what; we can apply this detector definition to the characteristic curves to stock options just as well as to radio detectors. The eerie thing about it is that the "At Expiration Diagrams" of CALL options look pretty much like the diagrams for diode detectors!

An option is a contract that gives its owner the right to buy or the right to sell a fixed quantity of an underlying security at a specific price within a certain time constraint. Of course, to get such a deal, one must pay a price; nothing is free in this world including the markets. For example, suppose that you wish to buy 100 shares of stock in XYZ company in a month or so when you'll have the cash. However, you are thinking (guessing) that the market will be going up between now and then. You have the choice to buy an option now with an expiration date several months out paying a small percent of the stock purchase price to buy the option. At expiration of the option, given that the stock value is higher, you can chose to buy the 100 shares of the stock at the strike price of the option when you

bought the option. If the stock went down over that period, you would not exercise your option but lose only the amount paid for the option contract.

Figure 4 denotes an at expiration diagram for a CALL option for a given stock at a given strike price. Here's how you write down what you wanted, given that you went ahead with it:

Buy1 XYZ 2-month 20$ call at $1.00.

You bought 1 stock option of XYZ company for 100 shares at the strike price of $20 for $100, or 1$ for each share. If you stock goes down you will not exercise your option and you'll lose $100. If the stock went from $20 to $25 per share at expiration then you'd have the right to exercise the option contract and buy the 100 shares of XYZ at $20 per share. You total gain would then be 100*25 or $2,500 but you'd only pay $2,000 for the stock.

So what's the dotted line in the graph? It's the curve at the beginning of the contract. Over time the dotted line comes down to align with the solid hockey-stick at expiration curve.

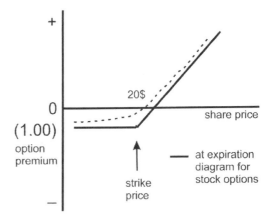

Figure 4

So there you have it. Different fields of endeavor often have a somewhat common basis in math. A detector can be a device designed to detect the presence of a particular object or substance and to emit a signal in response.

My Favorite Regen Receiver
Chip Olheiser, W7AIT

Crystal sets are fun, but my very first radio was the Span Master regenerative receiver Knight Kit. As a 12 year old, I had no experience soldering and sort of made a mess out of the wiring, but it worked. Since then I learned to solder, and have built and used two more regenerative receiver kits, the Ten Tec 1253 and the MFJ-8100K World Band Short Wave Radio. This article is about these kit radios, some regen term definitions and a little about how they work. For a surprising conclusion, I tell which of the three works best for me and why.

Regen Definitions

Regen: Regenerative design involving feedback, adjustable by the operator.

Regeneration Gain: Properly adjusted regeneration provides for gains up to 100 and perhaps higher.

Feedback: Typically the return (or feeding back) of the output to the input of an amplifier.

Oscillation: Controlling feedback produces oscillation. Too much results in Howls and Squeals. Not enough and the receiver sounds dead. Some practice is required to get it just right.

No AGC: Automatic gain control. Both Crystal Sets and regens have no AGC and are subject to fading / rising signals.

Active Device: A vacuum tube, transistor or integrated circuit; all require power from a battery or power supply. Regens require some sort of power vs. crystal sets that are usually self powered by the radio waves received.

Advantage: Regens rival superhets for sensitivity.

A Bit of History: Regens were used extensively aboard German U-Boats in WW II; Allied forces used them also; and, they devised methods to track down the U-boats by searching for the oscillating signal generated by those regens.

Ten Tec 1253
This is a transistor regen receiver covering selected SWL bands. Has band switch, a regen control, volume control, fine tuning and a main tuning dials. Requires +12 VDC. Performance is good when using a decent antenna. Mine is currently connected to my 9 foot high, 60 foot long front yard wire. An experienced operator can easily copy shortwave stations and amateur radio (ham) CW and SSB transmissions. The set is very sensitive, rivaling some superhets. Selectivity and repeatability are poor. The rig is prone to howls and squeals.

MFJ-8100K World Band Receiver
It's a transistor regen receiver covering selected SWL bands. Has band switch, regen control, volume control, and main tuning dial with Vernier fine adjust. Requires +12 VDC and headphones or an amplifier when using speakers. Performance is excellent when connected to a good antenna. Mine is currently sharing my antenna with the Ten TEC outlined above. A beginning novice operator can easily copy shortwave stations and ham CW and SSB. The set is very sensitive. Selectivity and repeatability are very good. The set is not prone to Howls and Squeals due to advanced but straightforward design additions.

Page 109

Knight Span Master

This is a two tube regen receiver covering from the broadcast band through 30 MHz. It features a band switch, regen controls, volume control, band spread and a main tuning dials, 110 VAC supply, and speaker. Performance is excellent connected to a good antenna. Mine was at 40 feet high and 50 feet long. An experienced operator can easily copy the AM broadcast band, shortwave stations and ham CW and SSB signals. The set is very sensitive rivaling some superhets. Selectivity and repeatability are poor. Very prone to Howls and Squeals.

Best of the Three:

Keeping in mind I built, tested and used all three of these regen receivers for several years, my favorite performer is the MFJ-8100K. Why? Simply put, this unit does not suffer from the squeal and howl problem. Additionally, tuning is smooth due to the vernier shaft tuning capacitor and requires no separate band spread control. On a scale of 0 to 10, I give the MFJ a 9, the Span Master an 8, and the Ten Tec a 6. Unfortunately, the Ten Tec is plagued with Squeals and Howls and additional scratchy potentiometer sounds by trying to pass RF over the wipers.

Simple Regen Block Diagram: Slanted arrows indicate operator controls.

The first block shows an optional radio frequency preamplifier, used to add gain, if necessary. If added, it helps in suppressing radiation (out the antenna) from the main regen circuit, which is inherently an oscillator.

The regen block is the heart of the receiver. Here several different actions are going on. Operator must set / compensate for band conditions, signal fading, strong nearby stations, BFO action if trying to detect CW or SSB, and the overall amount of oscillation required. Too little and receiver sounds totally dead. Too much and squeals and howls will drive you out of the room. Set just right results in great AM detection and good audio. Adjusting the frequency of the regen assists in receiving amateur radio CW and SSB (single side band audio) reception

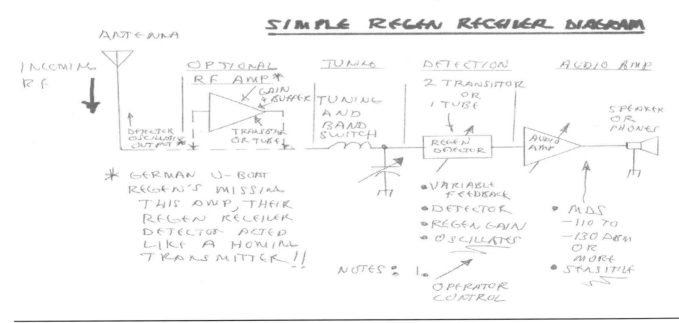

Rat Radio
by Ken Ladd

After my friend Cob Burandt and his buddies finished their rat rod he said "the true sign of a rat rod is not having much behind the garage when you're done". I saw a primer gray rat rod at a show with a bumper sticker the read SCREW SHINNY.

I went into this radio project with goal of using what was lying around and not buying anything unless I just had to. I bought an MRL 2 xtal kit and a one tube radio kit from Elmer Osterhoudt in the early 1970's. When the B battery went dead I boxed up the one tube. The xtal set saw limited use with an attic antenna at our previous house.

That all changed last year. While visiting my mother I found a forlorn wooden shotgun shell case in a shed. I cleaned it up being careful not to make it glitzy. I made a hinged cover with a plywood scrap but had to buy some hinges. I made a lid restraint with a toilet flapper valve chain.

I used a surplus drawer pull to open the lid. I mounted two magnetic latches (had to buy one). I mounted the one tube on the left side of the lid and mounted the xtal set in a cutout on the right. I used chain from a toilet flapper valve to restrain the lid when it is open.

I bought some semi rigid foam which I lined the bottom of the case. I made cutouts for the plug in coils, spare xtals, tubes and batteries. Three nine volt batteries rest in a metal Band-Aide box (B battery). I made a one cell holder from a two cell holder for the A supply. I have a small V-8 can that I might slip over it (juice to run the tube).

Oh yeah, I had to replace the tube when I stupidly switched the A and B leads (it was real bright for an instant).

Using a fifty foot antenna the xtal set brought in local stations. Using Brandees phones I picked up 690, 770, 830, 980, 1400 and 1500. Brush phones or sound powered ones would do better. I added posts and alligator clips so I can use a diode or a cat whisker.

The one tube brought these and more local stations but the shortwave amazed me. There was WWV, Family Radio, Radio Havana and foreign language stations. I also heard some ham sideband.

It is a thrill to sit quietly and listen. It brings back memories of the letters that Elmer sent with each order.

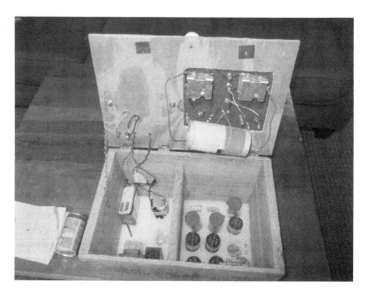

Page 111

Xtal Corner: Member Correspondence 2015

Queen Mum and Phil....
Thought you might like to see what an MK84 kit looks like with a 0.5 X 4.00 in. ferrite rod antenna. I wound it with 60 turns of #22 enamel wire, as you did on the Mini, Phil. I bought the nylon assortment kit from you for the bolts and clamps to hold the ferrite rod. In addition to the 4 inch rod, I bought an additional nylon screw and washer from a hardware store to fasten the main tuning cap more securely and a 6-32X1/8 screw to fasten the ground

lug to the cap frame. I also bought 4-40 bolts and nuts as fasteners along the back edge of the pc board. The only thing I have to to do now is blacken the screw heads on the front panel, and take one or two turns off the ferrite rod. Because of

the extra length, there is a little more inductance which moved a few of the stations at the top of the band out of reach with the tuning cap. But, other than that...THIS RADIO REALLY WORKS WELL!!!

Thanks much, Doug Howe

Phil ---
Several months ago, I built an RX3 ultrasound unit with the 12-inch parabolic dish. There are plenty of bats here in San Antonio, but during the past few weeks they have been flying around the street lights in large numbers. My wife and I get a big kick out of listening to them, most of which are Mexican free-tail bats. One of the interesting things that we've observed is that they emit a series of clicks; however, we've noticed that the frequency of these clicks often increases suddenly. Presumably, the frequency of their clicks increases when they lock onto an insect. Amazing stuff.Don Smith
San Antonio, Texas

Yup. You sure are in Bat Country. I ran across an interesting article about a year ago, wherein researchers mapped the flights of bats during hunting and recorded their clicking. It turns out that if they skim the water in a lake hunting for food, they give up if the water surface is rough due to wind, since the radar pulse (so to speak) that they send out comes back scrambled. Makes sense. Nice to hear from you. Phil, W0XI

Hello:
I would like to know the full range of capacitance of your 365 PF air tuning capacitor. I am guessing the minimum capacitance is around 10 PF but would like to really know the actual capacitance. I am planning and looking forward on making a crystal radio receiver as a project for some of my grandsons which was a project I had when in my younger years that brought me great excitement. Thanks! Steven W. Brown WB3DYZ

Hello Steven,
I just measured two of them

min 20   max 402
min 22   max 398 pf

This is pretty typical and of course, being mechanical each piece will vary a bit. I used my BK Precision C meter to check them; this too has a bit of variation.
73, and enjoy Phil Anderson, W0XI

From Ron Sindric:

Sorry if I seem to be excited about something small. But, here are some pix of my first attempt to construct a crystal radio from scratch. I worked on the detector some time ago, but never got around till now to put it all together. When it warms up it will be time to install an end-fed long wire antenna, lightning arrestor and stress relief to compensate for wind-induced wire and support tree movement. Note that I used Euro-style terminal strips to create an open design which will allow me to play with different wiring options for the radio. If I go to a carborundum crystal in the detector, I'll have to add a bias voltage. I am kicking around the idea of adding a small solderless prototyping board if I decide to play with biases, amps, etc. What might not be showing is the copper plate that runs the entire bottom of the breadboard. This plate is attached to the **GROUND** connection and serves as a **GROUND PLANE** for the radio.

I might build my next one into some other odd-yet-artistic wooden box. I also need to get MUCH better at winding coils by hand including large spiderweb detection coils and paired loose-coupled coils all in the name of making my radios more selective. Suggestions for future designs are welcome !

Noticeably absent is the tuning capacitor(s). I am still working on getting these.

I went out and scrounged some local thrift stores and will send pix of what I found. The local hardware store was a good source too.

I am sure the ideas I am passing along below are things already known by Crystal Radio Builders. Please forgive my ramblings:

I will make my next radio ground plane from trimmed and flattened sections of Aluminum pop cans.

The paper "tubes" I sometimes use for coil forms can be a bit fragile. Before I start winding the

coil, I mix water with carpenter's glue and paint it on both the inside and outside of the tube. After the glue dries, sometimes I spray the outside of the tubes with matte clear spray paint. The matte helps a small bit keep the wire in place as I hand-wind the coils. For small coils, my local thrift store is a good source for wooden sewing thread spools.

Cheers for now, Ron Sindric
a.k.a. Cornelius Blissripper-Sparrowcake Stochastic Steam Archaeologist and Armadillo Yodeling Instructor

From Anthony Dunn:
Will a brass screw load my xtal coil?
"My latest radio has a spider-web coil which is mounted by a brass screw in the center. A friend of mine is of the opinion that the conductive brass screw, although non-ferric, is introducing unwanted loading to the coil. What are your thoughts on that? Thanks!"

Two thoughts: 1) depends upon the size of the screw and 2) simply replace the brass screw with a nylon one. We sell small assortments of nylon hardware; see our website, www.midnightscience.com

Many sets have used a metal rod to tune the main coil of a set and paralleled that with a fixed capacitor. As the metal rod is pushed into the inside of the coil, the inductance of the coil, over all, is reduced. It is true that the Q (sharpness) of the tuned circuit is reduced too; and as such the tuning selectivity is reduced. One thing you can do to check your coil and brass screw is to tune in a station, then replace the brass screw with a nylon or plastic screw and then check if the station is still tuned in. If it is, the brass isn't affecting the circuit much. If it requires you to retune the set using the variable capacitor, but only by a small fraction of rotating the knob, then the effect of the brash screw is only slight (so don't worry about it). Nice to hear from you. Phil, WØXI.

Thanks Phil! I'll try the experiment as soon as my nylon hardware gets here. (Had a hunch, so I went ahead and ordered some from you.)
Anthony L Dunn

From Dean Lewis, W9WGV
Folks:
Four questions, if you wouldn't mind:

1. what's the difference between the Infinite Impedance Detector and the JFET Detector? Which works best?

The infinite detector preserves a bit more audio gain and fidelity.

2. Are either of them frequency-sensitive? (I

sometimes assemble xtal sets for shortwave frequencies.)

No. However, their high input impedance preserves the bandwidth of your LC circuit for HF.

3. What's the capacitance range of the trimmer cap used in your XS-402 Little Wonder Crystal Radio Kit?

50 to 200 PF

4. May I purchase a couple of these trimmer caps?
Tnx es vy 73;

I just finished my CIGAR BOX TUBE RADIO POWER SUPPLY. The P/S provides 1.5, 3.0, 4.5, 6.0 vDC from "D-cells" for tube filaments and 9, 18, 27, 36, 45, 54, 63, 72, 81, 90 vDC from snap-top 9 volt transistor radio batteries for plate and grid voltages.

It is a bit crude. But I am only a rookie at this wood-working stuff. Finishing touches in the form of labels are the only thing yet to be added. Hope you like the pix, Ron Sindric

Hello Patricia
I've been trying to find an answer to what I'd think would be a simple question. Folks I've written have replied with "don't know" up to and including "too complicated and not worth my time to investigate". So, I'd thought I'd give you and the technical staff at the Xtal Set Society a shot at it. Here goes ...

There are lost of pages on the Internet that discuss how to make air core and toroid baluns. The one issue that none seem to discuss is how many turns of wire you wind onto the core.

I want to make a 9:1, air core, balun for a couple of antennas. One is a random length antenna (approx 100 feet) that is up in the air. The other is a 200 to 300 foot antenna that is strung across, and insulated from, the ground (far end of this antenna is *NOT* connected to ground through a 500 Ω resistor). Both antennas have been used quite successfully on the long- medium and short waves. My question is: How many turns of wire to (initially) wind on the core to make the balun?

Looking forward to your comments and thoughts ...
John

John,

One source for "technical stuff" that is often overlooked is the ole Amateur Radio Handbook..........
most any edition....Mine is 2004 but these don't change much.

Look in the index for unums and baluns...........

A "balun" (balanced to unbalanced) is a device that matches a source to a load or a load to a source, wherein one is unbalanced and one is balanced. A popular example is coax (from a transmitter) feeding a dipole antenna. The Dipole is balanced and the coax is unbalanced. This type of balun is useful in that it "matches" the source and load and prevents current from returning back to a transmitter.

Another confusing piece of equipment - but very handy for those in the know - is the common mode choke (CMC). This device is often used to reduce noise from a source that would otherwise add noise to a driven load.

I'm way behind on a number of projects time wise right now so don't have time to write a paper on these.

I may be forced to look at your question, since I am trying to reduce the level of HF noise coming into my station which consists right now of an Elecraft K3, P3, and SteppIR vertical. One solution is to use a Beam antenna......but my space is restricted in distance and height (city restriction above 33 feet!).

I may try fiddling with a Beverage which has directional characteristics (pattern) and hence would reduce the noise received from the back side of the pattern and as such reduce the total noise received by the antenna.
Later, Phil, W0XI

Scrap Pile Radio
Ken Ladd

Imagine for a moment that it is the dead of winter and you are in a remote cabin in Canada in the early days. You slip your headphones on and make an adjustment or two on the crystal set you just finished building and you hear someone singing Annie Laurie. John Rowland's (1892 to 1972) did just that as he described in his 1947 book Cache Lake Country.

I read his book about 40 years ago and finally got around to building the radio he described. A radio engineer drew up a plan for him and provided a set of headphones and a diode detector. He left it up to John and his friends to find all of the other materials. These included foil from a tea box to build the sliding variable capacitor and wire from an engine ignition coil that they found when the snow shoed to an abandoned mine site.

I used .010 aluminum instead of foil and picked up on the theme of "scrap pile" concept. The only items that I purchased were brass thumb tacks and 8 screws. The plates of the capacitor are mounted at 45 degrees which allow for finer tuning. I used a 1n34A and for looks a steel galena crystal that I bought from Elmer Osterhoudt back in the day. There was a typo in the book which called for 166 turns on the coil which should have been 116. There was also a dimensional error and the diagram was also incorrect and incomplete. I used hardwood floor scraps for the rail and slider. After I glued the slider scraps together it was bowed and too thick so I ground it down on the concrete patio. I used pastry packaging to insulate the capacitor.

As expected the set is not very selective. Operating it here in Minneapolis makes it hard to judge the sensitivity. Mother Earth News republished the plan but I doubt it was ever built until now.

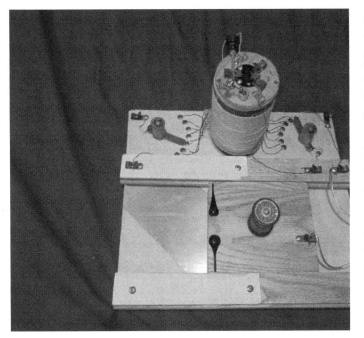

Hello. Thanks for the cool web site.
My grandson and I are wondering if, instead of using the normal type diodes, whether anyone has tried using some of the modern-day LED light diodes that are found in so many homes today for use in lighting. Great to know in the event of an emergency when no other 'normal' parts are available for making a broadcast band radio. Or, do they not work? If you post this, we'd be most interested in the responses.
Thank you, Mark St. Augustine, Florida

Hi Mark,
The crystal diodes, like the 1N34, are germanium, and as such start to conduct at (~.3V) at a lower voltage than regular contact diodes such as the popular 1N914. LEDs have a much higher conduction start and as such are not used for crystal sets since the AM radio signals generally are not strong enough to overcome this voltage threshold.

However - there is always an however - if you are willing to bias the LED with a **battery** and resistor.....it will indeed work in a crystal set. Crystal sets in the 1920s and 30s often used a piece of carbon and a needle as the detector; but, in that case they often biased it with some sort of battery. Today, you could use an solar panel as a small voltage source and then use the above larger threshold diodes.

Hope that is helpful. Several of our newsletter writers have outlined how to use solar panels in this way, as I recall within the last year. You can purchase backorders of most of our newsletters. Enjoy!

Hello-
I purchased (2) 365 PF Capacitor's your you for my AM loop antenna that I am building. This was sale # 34960 I am a relative newbie in loop antennas but learning a lot as I read and build. I need some guidance please on how to properly wire up this capacitor. I read the instructions and other material on this and need to ensure I am doing this right.

I have the two wire ends which I need to connect to the capacitor. I thought I needed to connect one wire end to one of the four lugs at the bottom of the capacitor (this must be soldered) and then the other end of the wire to either the front panel or the base (bottom) using a 6/32 screw. However and this is where I am confused your instructions say to attach one wire to either the front panel or base of the capacitor.. It does not mention to attach any wire to one of the for lugs. Maybe it is assumed you have to do this. I am thinking perhaps that capacitors can designed differently thus the needs for different wiring hookups. Any advice or guidance would be appreciated. David Turnick

Hello David,
The Xtal Set Society and xtal set builders use the dual gang as an antenna tuner. How the mag loop guys use it for tuning a mag loop may be different. However, the following may be helpful: The frame of the dual gang cap and 1/4 inch shaft sticking out the front are shorted to both rotor sections of the dual gang. Hence, to connect to the rotors you must connect a wire to the frame of the capacitor.

Here you can use one of the bottom three holes, threaded for a 6-32 screw with a solder lug under the head of the screw or one of the two threaded 6-32 holes at either side of the top of the front of the frame (where the shaft comes out).

The stators of the two capacitors are NOT connected together and each is isolated from the frame. Connect to either one of the set of stator plates by soldering a wire to the solder lug on either side of the selected section.

I suspect that the leads coming from the dual gang stators go to the two coils of the mag loop but am not sure; I have not experimented with mag loops.

A note of caution. Many callers have asked us what voltage our dual-gang caps can handle. The reason for this is that it has been said that mag loop antennas can create very high voltage when hi power is applied. Our caps only have 15 mils separation between plates, which according to Passion's Law would indicate air breakdown (arching) at somewhere around 300 volts. I

have seen some a few mag loop antennas designed for high power with capacitor tuning plates that are quite widely separated. Hope this is helpful. 73

From Gary Thorne:
Here are some sets I have been working on. I will send you copies of a couple articles I wrote. You can go to our club website and view stuff also: k9zev.org
I will show your newsletters at my table for our Hamfest if that is ok? Thanks

A question for "Grandpa Phil":

What are the real differences of the different grades of variable capacitors, relating to Xtal set use? Is it worth the trouble and expense to search out a "holy grail" capacitor, with the ceramic insulators, extra wiper contacts, and fancy plate shape? Thanks! Anthony L Dunn

Hi Anthony,

Depends upon what your desires are. The regular caps that we sell are pretty good but not mint...........Mint, or "best" has to do with the Q of the capacitor and how it is paralleled with a coil for the resonant circuit.

For really weak signal work and very narrow bandwidths, one likes to get the best Q for both the capacitor and coil in the tuned circuit. Since the antenna circuit already has loss primarily due to the real impedance of your ground, there is no reason to use the most expensive capacitors in that part of the circuit.

The very sensitive crystal sets use high impedance crystals or detection circuits. One can poor boy that down by using a JFET transistor as the detector. That way the audio circuit of the set does not drag down the Q of the tuned circuit...........that would likely use Litz wire on a low-loss form in parallel or otherwise with a capacitor that has nylon or similar standoffs (to hold he rotor and stationary plates apart) rather than the standard phenolic PCB sections like you see in our traditional 365 uuf variable caps. Most hobbyists are unaware of the difference and are often first time builders...........so that's ok.

Basically, you'll get that last 10% of the signals you couldn't get with the standard caps. But, that last 10% will be costly. Same old tradeoffs in life.

If you are interested in the technical details, search for Ben Tongue's website.................on super optimizing a set for the last 10 percent.

You can get some insight into this process from a paper I wrote for ARRL back in September 2008 in their QEX magazine.

Ed Asked
:
1) If I can't find enough varnished wire for wrapping coils, is there a way I can varnish bare wire?
2) Does the wire for the oatmeal box radio have to be solid wire, or can I use stranded?
3) Does wire for any coil have to be copper?
4) And can I use # 6 aluminum wire from a piece of triplex service cable for an antenna? Thanks. Ed

Hi Ed

1 & 3) I don't know how manufacturers coat enamel onto wire. Magnet wire "also called enameled wire" is a copper or aluminum wire coated with a very thin layer of insulation. It is used in the construction of transformers, coils, etc and other applications that require tight coils (i.e. no spacing between the turns) of insulated wire. Copper wire has less loss than aluminum so should be used unless the length of the wire is short. Copper is preferred for coils. By the way, one can use a soldering iron to "boil off" the enamel in order to solder the ends to a terminal, etc.
2) Both solid and stranded wire work well for AM band crystal sets. Many strands of enamel wire woven together - often called Litz wire - are preferred for crystal sets, due to the skin effect, wherein for high frequencies - particularly the HF AM band - the current flows only on or near the surface of the wire. No current flows at the center of those wire strands. As such, Litz wire has a lower resistance loss than solid wire and is therefore used if you wish to make a more efficient and weak signal crystal set.
4) #6 wire would work ok but is heavy. From AM band - 500 to 1500 kHz - #22 or #26 wire will work as well but is not nearly as heavy. Phil, W0XI, at the Xtal Set Society.

92051818R00069

Made in the USA
San Bernardino, CA
28 October 2018